A Project Approach to
Language Learning

Linking Literary Genres and Themes in Elementary Classrooms

Katherine Luongo-Orlando

Pembroke Publishers Limited

To Issabella Victoria,
may your life always be filled with the magic of learning and the wonder of discovery

To Matt,
for the book talks and support

In memory of my mother Victoria, the spirit that guides me

© **2001 Pembroke Publishers**
538 Hood Road
Markham, Ontario, Canada L3R 3K9
www.pembrokepublishers.com

Distributed in the U.S. by Stenhouse Publishers
477 Congress Street
Portland, ME 04101
www.stenhouse.com

We acknowledge the financial support of the Government of Canada through the Book Publishing Industry Development Program (BPIDP) for our publishing activities.

Canadian Cataloguing in Publication Data

Luongo-Orlando, Katherine
   A project approach to language learning : linking literary genres and themes in elementary classrooms

Includes index.
ISBN 1-55138-128-1

1. Language arts (Elementary). 2. English language – Study and teaching (Elementary). 3. Project method in teaching. I. Title.

LB1576.L86 2001   372.6′044   C00-932639-1

Editor: Jennifer Drope
Cover Design: John Zehethofer
Typesetting: JayTee Graphics

Printed and bound in Canada
9 8 7 6 5 4 3 2 1

Contents

Chapter 3 — Studying Traditional Folklore: Mythical and Legendary Short Stories That Feature Characterization and Heroes *57*

Chapter 4 — Creating Poetry: The Production of a Classroom Anthology That Highlights Literary Forms and the Environment *75*

Chapter 6 — Recounting Oral Stories: Storytelling That Celebrates Literature and the Cultures of the World *121*

Chapter 7 — Assessment and Evaluation   *133*

Foreword

Children have a natural curiosity for language and a fascination with projects that challenge them to use a range of talents, skills and materials in creative ways. Introducing young people to the imaginative world of literature through projects enables them to explore language via rich interconnected learning activities that enhance their experience with texts. Each reading experience leads to a new encounter with an array of genres, characters, settings, plots, ideas and facts that make up the world of print. These literature experiences can, in turn, inspire young people to produce a variety of innovative works that enrich their learning.

Over the years, I have used children's literature to develop creative language activities and projects for my students. The pages of this book are filled with a rich selection of written, visual, oral and dramatic responses produced by children from diverse backgrounds and different ability levels. This book is an effort to help teachers in elementary classrooms implement learning projects that explore a variety of children's literature, connect literary genres and themes, and build knowledge and skills through language activities that can be used throughout the curriculum. The practical suggestions are meant to provide open invitations and inspiration for teachers who want to share literature with students and provide rich language experiences that build on children's natural curiosity, imaginative powers and creative skills. By engaging in the integrated learning activities that make up the projects in each chapter, teachers and students will be able to produce complex final products that instill pride and call for celebration.

About This Book

A Project Approach to Language Learning focuses on building knowledge and skills through extensive projects that explore various literary genres and themes. Knowledge and skills are introduced and developed through a series of learning activities that lead to the creation of a special final product (e.g., a poetry anthology, a thematic newspaper etc.). Each project culminates in a learning celebration that involves the entire class and often members of the school community.

The book concentrates specifically on projects that explore the following genres — novels, picture books, traditional folklore, poetry, non-fiction and storytelling. The themes highlighted in each chapter are used as vehicles for exploring the various genres. These themes are based on universal concepts in literature, and include: Relationships,

OVERVIEW OF LANGUAGE LEARNING PROJECTS				
Chapter Title	Genre(s)	Theme	Project	General Knowledge/Skills
Examining the Novel	Novels	Relationships	Create response activities for a Novel Exhibition and Museum Collection Display.	• Understand the characteristics of novels. • Identify basic elements of story. • Read and respond to novels in a variety of ways.
Publishing Picture Books	Picture Books	Interdependence	Produce a picture book for a Publisher's Fair and Literary Awards Presentation.	• Understand the characteristics of picture books. • Investigate various conventions for writing a story. • Apply knowledge of story elements to writing a picture book. • Use the stages of the writing process.
Studying Traditional Folklore	Myths & Legends	Heroes	Write myths and legends for a Folklore Convention and Television Talk Show.	• Understand the characteristics of myths and legends. • Extend knowledge of story elements (especially character). • Apply knowledge of story elements and narrative structure to other genres.
Creating Poetry	Poetry	Environment	Write poems and create a classroom anthology for a Poetry Reading.	• Understand the characteristics of different forms of poetry. • Read and respond to poetry in a variety of ways. • Produce poetry using various forms and conventions.
Investigating Non-Fiction	Non-Fiction	Past and Present	Use non-fiction research to prepare a newspaper for a Newspaper Release Press Party.	• Understand characteristics of non-fiction and newspapers. • Conduct research using non-fiction resources. • Use steps in the research process to gather information and develop inquiry skills. • Present research findings in the form of news items (e.g., report).
Recounting Oral Stories	Storytelling	Multiculturalism	Prepare an oral story for a Storytelling Festival.	• Listen to stories from a variety of sources. • Select a story to tell. • Produce a story map. • Tell stories aloud in an engaging way.

Interdependence, Heroes, the Environment, the Past and Present, and Multiculturalism. The themes that are offered to support the genre studies described in each chapter can easily be replaced by others that reflect the interests of the children and the curriculum. The overview chart included here highlights the general knowledge and skills addressed in each project.

The projects are designed to build knowledge and skills through activities that nurture children's development in the language areas and beyond. Ideas for integrating authentic reading, writing, speaking and listening activities and building literacy into all aspects of the program are included. By providing opportunities for students to demonstrate their understanding of literature and non-fiction in a variety of ways, young people are able to use language for real purposes.

The language learning projects described in this book provide opportunities for students to work individually, in groups and as a class. They can be used with students in the late primary, junior and intermediate grades. A range of instructional strategies are included so that teachers can select, modify and tailor each project to meet the needs of their students and their program. The learning activities provided are supported by classroom experiences, student samples and blackline masters that can be reproduced for student use.

Using This Book

The activities in the chapters in this book have been organized according to the progression of knowledge and skills required to complete each project. Many of the projects build on the learning experiences in previous chapters. However, the projects presented in each chapter do not necessarily have to be approached in sequence — they can also be implemented separately or in a different order.

In Chapter 1, students are introduced to the basic elements of story through novels related to a theme such as Relationships. Learners develop knowledge and language skills by engaging in a variety of response activities.

In Chapter 2, learners use picture books dealing with a theme such as Interdependence to examine how story elements and aspects of narrative writing are constructed in children's literature. Students then have the opportunity to apply knowledge and language skills to the creation of their own theme-related picture books.

In Chapter 3, learners explore aspects of narratives, especially characterization, in greater depth by studying traditional folklore focusing on myths and legends related to a theme such as Heroes. Students are then encouraged to apply knowledge and language skills to produce their own myths and legends.

In Chapter 4, learners study poetry related to a theme such as the Environment and examine the literary devices, styles and formats used to produce different types of poems. Students then apply knowledge and language skills specific to the genre to their own works of poetry to produce a thematic classroom anthology.

In Chapter 5, students learn to use non-fiction sources to conduct research on a topic related to a theme such as the Past and Present. Learners build knowledge and language skills to present research findings in the form of a thematic newspaper.

In Chapter 6, students participate in storytelling experiences related to a theme such as Multiculturalism. Learners are able to build knowledge and language skills as they prepare oral stories to share at a storytelling festival.

Each chapter has been divided into the following sections:

- INTRODUCTION
  - provides an overview of the chapter's genre, suggested theme and learning project

- INTRODUCING THE GENRE/THEME
  - provides background information about the genre and theme, as well as a rationale for instruction

- KNOWLEDGE/SKILL COMPONENTS
  - highlights particular knowledge and skills that are developed throughout the project

- INTRODUCTORY ACTIVITIES
  - includes activities that help students acquire background knowledge and skills to complete the project

- CORE ACTIVITIES
  - includes activities that engage students in different stages of the language learning project

- LEARNING CELEBRATION
  - describes the celebration of learning that takes place following project completion

- EXTENSION ACTIVITIES
  - lists activities that can extend the learning experience

- CONCLUSION
  - offers final thoughts on the genre, theme, knowledge and skills of the project

Throughout each project, students are encouraged to use a variety of theme-related texts to work through the various activities. The text sets used may include trade books, reference materials, newspapers, magazines, novels, picture books, short stories, poems and/or traditional folklore that provide models for students' work. Collections of published materials, many organized around the themes featured in this book, are offered in resource lists at the end of the book.

By engaging in projects that allow them to experience different types of literature and to create their own works of art, students can become part of a community of learners who share in literary experiences that engage the imagination and open up the world of creativity. Together may you delight in the learning activities, marvel at the work produced and celebrate children as authors, illustrators, poets, non-fiction writers and storytellers.

CHAPTER ONE

Examining the Novel

Response activities that explore narrative
elements and relationships

The rich variety of novels available today serve as wonderful vehicles for
literary exploration and reading response. Novels have the power to
invite readers to enter the story world and experience the lives of the
characters in a profound way. As humans, our world is shaped by our
interactions with others. Young people are especially interested in this
facet of human life, making the theme of Relationships a suitable one to
explore through novels.

By engaging in response activities, readers can discover story
elements, themes and interrelationships featured in novels. Through
reading, discussion, writing and arts activities, students have the
opportunity to develop the ability to analyze the text, interpret ideas
related to the theme and make connections to their own lives. These
experiences can, in turn, contribute to cognitive development and
higher-level processes such as critical and creative thinking in readers
of all ages.

INTRODUCING THE GENRE/THEME

Using Novels as a Vehicle for Response

Creating a novel program is one of the most effective ways of inviting
young people to respond to literature. The very structure of a novel
enables students to engage in a variety of learning activities as they
interact with a text. Since novels are long and take time to work through,
readers cannot become acquainted with the entire book in a single
sitting. Time must be spent reflecting on the author's words, interpreting
story events and responding to the text in different ways in order to
make meaning. By expanding on the themes, issues and content of
novels, teachers can plan creative learning activities that aim to enrich
children's experiences with literature.

Creating Theme-Related Novel Text Sets

In order to create a novel text set, selections can be successfully
organized around a particular theme, such as Relationships. While
constructing a thematic collection, teachers should select novels based on
students' prior experiences with literature and their different reading
levels, abilities and interests. The selections may challenge, stimulate

and/or entertain students. Books with compelling plots, vivid characterizations and interesting language should be part of classroom theme collections. Multiple copies of the same novel should be available for group exploration. The text set might also include quality works of literature produced by different authors from all over the world. All books in the collection should contain authentic information and convey positive images of males, females and members of different racial, ethnic or cultural groups.

Novel collections can be organized around a variety of themes. Novels that deal with Relationships, such as those offered at the end of the book, are especially relevant to young people. Books based on friendships, families, school life and other related topics are within the readers' world of experience. Selecting novels that deal with social issues can help students understand aspects of more complex relationships and the realities of the human condition. Regardless of the theme chosen, novels should be rich with language, exemplify quality literature, model good writing and enrich the reading experience of children of all ages.

KNOWLEDGE/SKILL COMPONENTS

Placing novels at the centre of the language curriculum enables students to develop knowledge and language skills that are necessary to become effective readers. By reading and responding to novels in a variety of ways, such as those explained in this chapter, learners will be able to:

- Understand the characteristics of a novel;
- Identify story elements (i.e., plot, setting, characters, theme);
- Read novels for a variety of purposes (e.g., for enjoyment, to gain information, to develop skills etc.);
- Use different strategies to make sense of texts (e.g., reread to clarify meaning);
- Enjoy listening to novels read aloud, participate in shared reading experiences and read books independently;
- Reflect on reading material and make personal connections to their own life experiences;
- Respond to novels in a variety of ways (e.g., through discussion, writing, arts activities etc.) that extend their reading experience;
- Develop higher-level thinking skills (e.g., critical and creative thinking);
- Make inferences, judgements and predictions based on reading material;
- Interpret and analyze the features and content of a novel;
- Revisit texts to locate supporting details;
- Develop inquiry skills by raising questions and examining issues in novels;
- Construct meaning in personal and collective ways;
- Share individual opinions and insights with others;
- Use their imagination and creativity to respond to novels;
- Develop an appreciation for literature and enjoyment of reading.

The learning activities in this chapter are designed to allow students to explore novels related to a chosen theme, such as Relationships. The teaching strategies provided will help students read for meaning, identify the elements of story and understand the characteristics of a novel. Learners will then be able to respond to novels in a variety of ways and share their literary responses at a Novel Exhibition and Museum Collection Display.

INTRODUCTORY ACTIVITIES

Creating the Environment

Creating the proper learning environment is important when developing a novel program. The inviting atmosphere of a good classroom library can motivate students to read books. To accomplish this, establish a setting where young people can read and respond to novels in a variety of ways. Have the students create a reading corner complete with a rocking chair, pillows, sofa or rug to help create the right mood. Classroom libraries should feature a set of novels related to a chosen theme, such as Relationships. Invite the children to select their own novels that can be included in this collection.

In order to create an atmosphere that encourages students to explore literature and respond to novels in different ways, provide additional resources and learning materials that can extend children's reading experiences. Apart from book displays, a reading corner may include bulletin boards, posters, puppets, felt boards, headsets, tape recorders, stories on audiotape, materials for making books, as well as works of literature written, illustrated and published by the students themselves.

Introducing the Novel

To introduce the genre, share the collection of novels organized around a common theme, such as Relationships, with the class. Review several novels in the text set collection by reading book summaries, critical reviews, opening chapters and interesting parts aloud. Provide an opportunity for students to read, explore and discuss novels in the thematic collection individually, in pairs or in small groups.

After exploring books in the text set collection, challenge students to identify the characteristics of a novel. As a class, examine the format, layout and parts of a novel closely, brainstorm the different components and produce a list like the one shown here.

Once students understand the characteristics of this genre, they can begin exploring novels in the text set collection in more detail.

Characteristics of a Novel

A novel may:

- Be organized into chapters that have their own titles/heads.
- Contain a contents page outlining the various chapters in the book.
- Feature few, if any, illustrations.
- Be divided into different parts.
- Contain a prologue to the story.
- Have sequels that are based on the same characters, setting etc..

Exploring Novel Text Sets

Read-Aloud Experiences

There is no better way to demonstrate the wonderful appeal of a good novel than by reading it aloud. When children experience literature in this way, they learn to associate reading with pleasure and their interest in literature grows. Read-aloud experiences benefit young people by:

- Providing them with valuable information about the world;
- Enriching their vocabulary;
- Improving their listening skills;
- Expanding their use of oral language;
- Stimulating their imagination;
- Entertaining them.

When children are read to, they are often carried into a world of adventure, fantasy and make-believe. Sometimes the content is so compelling that it touches their lives deeply and awakens their sense of compassion, empathy and sensitivity to the world.

In order to develop children's interest in novels, read aloud to them everyday. Set aside regular periods for reading aloud, regardless of the grade level you teach. Children of all ages enjoy being read to. Select a novel that interests your students and read a chapter to them each period. Following a read-aloud event, provide opportunities for students to respond to the novel in literary discussions and other language experiences. Students themselves should also be encouraged to select their own novels and practise reading aloud to others. These experiences will extend their involvement, enjoyment and appreciation of literature.

Independent, Shared and Guided Reading

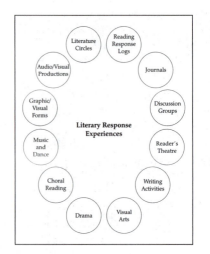

Students can also explore novels in the text set collection by selecting a book they are interested in and reading it independently, with a partner or in a small group. Providing time for pleasure reading in the classroom may convince young people that reading novels can be an enjoyable and rewarding experience. After interacting with books in a personal way, students may be eager to respond to the novels they have read by engaging in activities such as those illustrated in the diagram and explained further in this chapter.

CORE ACTIVITIES

Organizing a novel study can invite readers to experience literature and connect to the world of story in a focused way. Participating in a novel study challenges students to explore the characteristics of the genre, elements of story and aspects of the theme in detail. A novel study can be facilitated in a number of ways. Novels can be:

- Selected by the teacher;

- Selected by the students themselves (summarized briefly by the teacher before student selection);
- Assigned to the entire class;
- Assigned to a small group of students;
- Assigned to individual students;
- Used for guided reading experiences (supervised reading activity for short passages from the text).

To establish a novel study, try balancing these approaches in order to accommodate students' various reading levels, deal with differences in learners' reading abilities and incorporate students' individual interests. Once a novel study has been established, students can begin examining story elements and engaging in response activities.

Examining the Basic Elements of Story

After introducing novels to the students in a variety of ways, they should be ready to explore traditional aspects of literature, such as plot, setting, character and theme. By examining the basic elements of story in context, children's knowledge of novels will grow. Understanding these features will provide young people with a conceptual framework to structure their responses to literature.

Plot

Well-crafted novels are based on fascinating storylines that command the reader's attention. The events in a novel are arranged in sequence to form the plot. The plot of a story connects different elements together, including the characters and the setting.

To explore plot in detail, select a novel related to the chosen theme to read aloud to the class. During the read-aloud experience, ask students to recall incidents in the story and make predictions about upcoming events. Have children identify significant information in the novel that contributes to the plot development, such as:

- Opening events;
- Conflicts/problems;
- Major happenings in the story (highlights);
- Resolutions;
- Conclusion.

Learners can consolidate an understanding of the plot by identifying the main events in a novel, organizing them in sequence and writing a summary of the book on their own. Later, students can present the events in the form of a comic strip. Children may wish to produce plot summaries and comic strips for different chapters or parts of a novel by using a handout like the one presented on the following page.

Examining the Plot

Select a chapter or section from a novel in the theme collection that you have read or listened to. Read the selection carefully. Use one of the following sets of words to list the events in order. Write a summary of the novel's events using the sequence words you selected.

- First, then, also, next, finally
- First, next, after, later, last
- Starting, later, then, also, concluding with
- At the start, second, next, then, finally
- In the beginning, next, afterwards, later, at the end

Part A: List the important events in order using the sequence words.

_____

_____

_____

_____

_____

Part B: Write a paragraph describing the most important events in the chapter or section of the novel you selected.

_____

_____

_____

_____

_____

Part C: Produce a five-frame comic strip illustrating the main events of the chapter or section you selected from the novel.

Title: _____

Author: _____

Setting

Mary, Age 12

Sheri & Gita, Age 11

The settings of a novel include the places where the plot unfolds. They represent the world where the characters live. Students can develop an understanding of setting by examining the scenes where the novel takes place.

After reading a novel aloud, ask students to list the various settings in the story. Learners should begin with the opening scene and identify all the locations where the major actions or events happen in the novel. Ask students to note changes in setting by marking new locations with adhesive notes or other items of reference. Learners should try to determine the following information when observing the settings of a novel:

- The cities, countries, towns, villages or communities where the story takes place;
- Places of residence (i.e., homes, apartments);
- Places of work/business and recreation sites;
- Landmarks and important surroundings;
- Physical environment or scenery.

After identifying the different scenes in a novel, students can be challenged to recreate a setting or settings using visual arts techniques and materials. Class members can work cooperatively to produce a series of charcoal or pastel drawings, water color paintings or other artistic illustrations to depict scene changes in the novel, or students can work together in groups to create a travel brochure depicting a setting in the novel.

Character

Novels are often filled with dynamic characters that can transcend print and become part of a young reader's life. A skilled author has the power to develop characters that young people can relate to and grow to love. With each detail that readers discover about a character, a strong relationship begins to form between themselves and the important people in the story.

Students can develop an understanding of this story element by examining characters in the thematic collection. After reading the opening chapter of a novel to the class, discuss the characters and make a list of information the author reveals about each person in the book (e.g., appearance, gestures, habits, talents, skills, abilities, background etc.). Learners should try to recall specific information about each person introduced in the chapter by providing examples from the text.

By examining the author's description of the characters in a novel, young people will begin to understand what Ralph Fletcher refers to in his book *What a Writer Needs* as a character's private and public persona. To assist students in understanding these complex aspects of character:

- Share examples from novels that describe a character's appearance, personal accomplishments and biological background.
- Explain that these components are part of a character's public image.

- Ask readers to find examples and details from the text that reveal a character's emotions, habits, fears and strengths.
- Explain that these traits are part of a character's inner being or private life.

To consolidate young readers' understanding of character elements, provide them with the following learning activity:

- Ask students to select their favorite character from a novel.
- Distribute a sheet of blank paper to each student.
- Instruct students to fold the sheet in half.
- Have students brainstorm information revealed about the character in the novel (e.g., appearance, gestures, habits, talents, skills, abilities, background) on the back of the folded sheet.
- Challenge students to determine the aspects that describe the character's public and private life.
- Ask students to create a portrait of the character on the front page and write a brief description of the public persona (e.g., accomplishments, background etc.) beneath it.
- Have students write about the private life of the character (e.g., fears, emotions, habits, strengths etc.) on the inside page.
- Display the character profiles on a bulletin board entitled "The Character Hall of Fame."

Theme

As children interact with texts, most are able to identify characters, setting and plot correctly. However, many young readers struggle to understand the theme in a piece of writing. The theme is the central meaning or main idea of a story that often carries a universal message or lesson for the reader. The author may communicate the main idea in a clear or underlying way. By examining the problems, issues and lessons in a work of literature, young readers can learn to identify the theme in a novel.

In order to capture the essence of theme in literature, have students examine the novel text set and identify recurring images or main topics in the collection. After reviewing the collection of novels about Relationships, for example, the students may identify the following theme aspects or central meanings in the stories:

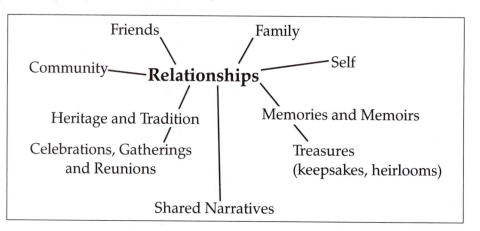

Once readers have identified the main idea(s) in the text set, have them create a collage or symbol that represents the theme(s) in the book collection or a novel itself. For a theme on Relationships, for instance, students can use photographs, words and real objects to create a collage, or design symbols that represent keepsakes, treasures, memoirs and other items related to Relationships.

Exploring Narrative Elements through Response

Once students understand the basic elements of story and are able to identify these traditional aspects of literature, they are ready to explore different forms of response.

There are many ways that readers can respond to literature. Traditional approaches to literature instruction focus on understanding narrative elements (plot, setting, characters, theme) through a literal examination of the text. In these classrooms, readers are often assigned comprehension questions and workbook exercises while reading a novel or another text.

In a response-based program, students construct meaning through their interactions with literature. Readers first respond to a text by reflecting on their emotions, attitudes, beliefs, interests and personal experiences and then, relate these to the work being studied. The ways in which readers identify with characters, interpret visual images, relate autobiographical experiences or construct the story world may vary. By providing opportunities for students to respond to reading through drama, writing, visual arts activities, discussions and other forms of response, teachers can help young people acquire a greater appreciation for literature. These experiences can promote higher-level thinking, improve literacy skills and enhance creativity too.

Many of the response activities outlined in this section involve cooperative learning. Before engaging in these learning experiences, students must establish social guidelines for participating in a group to ensure that all learners can share personal opinions, offer suggestions, present ideas and make other contributions. At the same time, teachers must affirm students' responses to a novel and assure readers that their impressions and ideas are valued and accepted by others. These conditions will help create a positive learning environment in a response-based literature program.

In order to engage students in a variety of response experiences, you may wish to try some of the following activities.

Discussions about Literature

Students benefit from opportunities to read and talk about literature. Through discussion, readers are able to express emotions, explore ideas and negotiate understandings of a novel. Discussions can begin with students sharing their initial interpretations of a story or describing the images and feelings they had during the reading experience. Students should be encouraged to record thoughts or issues as they read their novel. These notes can later be used as starting points for discussion.

Discussions about literature can take place in a variety of ways. These conversations may include:

- Interviews;
- Reading conferences/workshops;
- Free-association think alouds;
- Cooperative group jigsaws;
- Book talks;
- Literature circles;
- Class meetings;
- Whole-class panel discussions.

Depending on the activity, students may participate in discussions in pairs, small groups, or as an entire class.

Interviews

After reading a novel, have students work together in pairs to interview one another about the book. Prior to the interview, learners should generate a list of questions they want to ask their peers. These questions can be based on:

- The content of the novel (e.g., character relationships);
- The reading strategies used to understand the text;
- The author's writing style;
- Personal reactions/opinions;
- Related life experiences;
- Similar encounters with stories.

Composing questions beforehand will stimulate discussion and help students think and respond critically to a text. When answering questions during the interview, readers should elaborate, clarify or explain their responses fully by providing evidence from the novel. After reading the novel *Naomi's Road*, my students interviewed one another about theme aspects in the novel by exploring the complex relationships of the characters. Readers discussed the impact of World War II and Japanese internment in Canada on the family relationships in the book.

Reading Conferences/Workshops

Following a novel encounter, invite students to participate in a reading conference or workshop with you (the teacher) or another student. The purpose of the reading conference is not to provide a synopsis or plot summary but to critically analyze a text. When examining the different elements of story, students should revisit the novel, consider evidence presented in the text and explore other perspectives offered by conference partners. Readers can also share personal experiences and opinions of a novel.

While reading *Mieko and the Fifth Treasure*, my students held reading conferences to discuss the influence that other characters (parents, grandparents, teachers, friends etc.) had on the protagonist, Mieko, as she struggled through personal conflicts in the novel.

Free-Association Think Alouds

As readers interact with a novel, they can also participate in free-association think alouds, an oral language strategy developed by Patrick Dias. During the novel encounter, students express their ongoing thoughts and feelings as they read. The reading experience can be interrupted so the learner can express ideas or visual images. After reading a brief story segment or excerpt from a novel, the learner stops to share interpretations with others or verbalize his/her thoughts about a text. This strategy is particularly effective with developing and reluctant readers. During an independent reading period, I have worked with individual students to develop their reading habits using this technique.

Cooperative Group Jigsaws

The jigsaw technique can also be used effectively for literary discussions. In order to implement this strategy:

- Designate students to cooperative groups (home groups).
- Assign each member a different story element, topic or issue to examine in a novel (e.g., setting, language, characterization etc.).
- Invite the students with similar story elements, topics or issues to form new (expert) groups to discuss the focused subject matter.
- Ask students to rotate back to their original group to share their new insights on the novel with the other members.

My students used this strategy effectively to examine and discuss the relationships among family members, friends, members of society (e.g., marginalized groups such as the elderly) and other important people (e.g., authority figures) in the theme books.

Book Talks

Book talks can also be held to discuss a novel. To model this type of literary discussion:

- Select a novel in the text set collection.
- Summarize the events in the opening chapter to the students.
- Present the characters, setting and plot briefly.
- Read aloud dramatic segments from the book to the class.
- End the presentation at an interesting part of the story.
- Challenge the students to read the rest of the novel themselves.

After reading a novel they have selected, students may wish to engage in their own book talks about the text. During these book talks, learners can share their reading experiences, interpretations of the story and predictions about upcoming events.

Literature Circles

As readers interact with a novel they can participate in literature circles, a response technique described by Harvey Daniels in his book *Literature Circles: Voice and Choice in the Student-Centered Classroom*. Literature circles are small, temporary discussion groups comprised of students who have selected the same novel to read. The steps shown here can help facilitate these group conferences.

Facilitating Literature Circles

- Ask members to decide how far they will read (e.g., number of pages, chapters etc.) prior to the literature circle.
- Have each student assume responsibility for a different story element or role in the cooperative group (e.g., discussion director).
- Schedule time for independent reading.
- Have students take notes in a reading log or response journal during the reading event.
- Invite group members to share their notes and insights with others during the literature circle.

Afterwards, have students plan the next meeting by determining the amount of content to read. In order to examine story elements fully, learners should assume new roles that will focus their reading and guide the follow-up discussion. Participating in these student-led discussions enables readers to take control of their learning, explore different interpretations of texts and construct meaning with others.

Class Meetings

Class meetings can also be held to discuss literature. The purpose of a class meeting is to help readers explore and further develop their understanding of a novel in a large group. As students share their personal interpretations with others, they become aware of alternative viewpoints. By examining these various perspectives as a group, readers will either change their initial impressions or learn to defend their point of view. Students can justify an established position by providing examples from the novel to support their opinion. These experiences can increase students' involvement with a text.

Through class discussions, students not only share the process of interpretation and raise questions leading to deeper analysis, they also become aware of the reading strategies used by others to understand a text. While reading the novel *Bridge to Terabithia* to my students, I have often held class meetings to discuss the complex relationships in the book. In a large group discussion, the children and I analyzed family relationships (e.g., parenting styles), friendships and aspects of school life (e.g., social acceptance, bullying).

Whole-Class Panel Discussions

In whole-class panel discussions, students can share a variety of novels in the theme collection. After a group of students have finished reading a novel in the text set, readers provide a summary of the plot, characters, moral dilemmas and other interesting story details to the class. Following each group presentation, students pose questions to the panel members and ask them to share personal opinions, interpretations and related experiences. Following all of the presentations, participants can share common features in the texts, examine the authors' intentions and compare different writing styles of books in the theme collection.

Reading Response Logs

Another way to invite students to explore novels is through reading response logs, as outlined by Kooy and Wells in their book *Reading Response Logs: Inviting Students to Explore Novels, Short Stories, Plays, Poetry and More*. A response log is a notebook, binder or folder where readers can record their thoughts, reactions, questions, predictions and discoveries about a novel or other literary text in a variety of chosen formats. Students can record information on reading material in many ways, as shown in the box on this page.

Reading Response Log Entry Formats

- Lists
- Timelines
- Jot Notes
- Questions
- Graphs
- Diagrams
- Family Trees
- Paragraphs
- Predictions
- Reports
- Maps
- Letters
- Webs
- Reactions
- Articles
- Charts
- Diaries
- Plot Lines
- Scripts
- Posters
- Sketches
- Journal Entries
- Venn Diagrams
- Sociograms
- Illustrations

Through the use of a variety of response strategies, readers have the opportunity to interpret the basic elements of story in a novel collection, as well as to express their personal reactions to their reading. Graphic organizers such as Venn diagrams, character webs, plot lines, family trees and other visual models can be used effectively to synthesize information from a novel. Students' understanding of character relationships and other theme aspects can be revealed in labelled diagrams, illustrations, jot notes and paragraphs among others. A few reading response log strategies that have worked particularly well with my students are outlined below.

Positive-Negative Graphs
Readers can produce positive-negative graphs to illustrate the events that occur in a character's life, relationships with others, or the novel as a whole. In these graphic models, the tragedies and joys appear in sequence as they happen in the novel.

Organizing the plot developments in this way enables readers to make connections between the characters and the events that affect their lives and relationships. For example, after reading *The Belonging Place* by Jean Little, my students produced positive-negative graphs to summarize the events in young Elspet Mary's life. This visual model illustrates the impact of important plot developments (e.g., her parent's death) on the relationships that form in the novel (e.g., with guardians, family members, neighbors etc.).

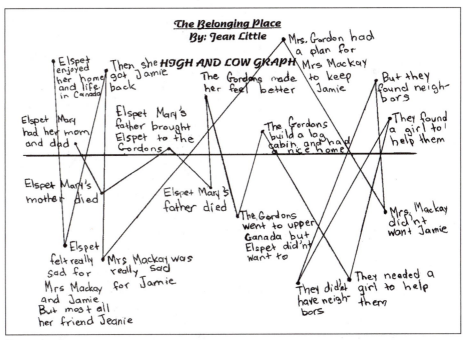

Faraz, Age 9

Sociograms

Sociograms offer another effective way to visually demonstrate the relationships among the characters in a novel. In order to create a sociogram, ask students to do the following:

- Print the main character's name in a large circle in the centre of the page.
- Record the names of lesser characters in smaller circles around the larger one.
- Decide on the type of relationship two characters share and demonstrate that relationship by using connectors. The following techniques can be used:
  - lines of varying lengths to show the proximity and closeness of the characters to one another;
  - a variety of lines, such as straight lines for family, jagged lines for enemies etc.;
  - words recorded along the lines to indicate the main character's relationship to the other characters in the book.

In the example shown, my student produced a sociogram to show the relationships among the characters in the novel *The Castle in the Attic* by Elizabeth Winthrop.

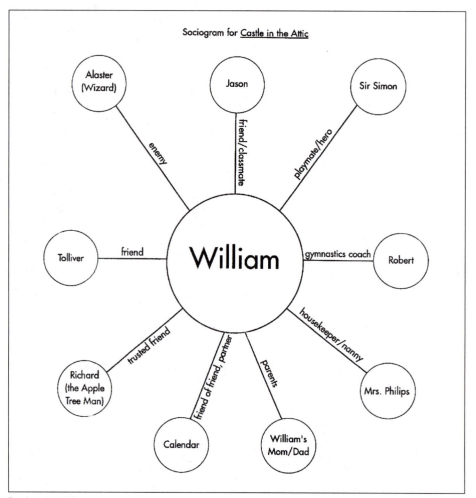

Jessica, Age 11

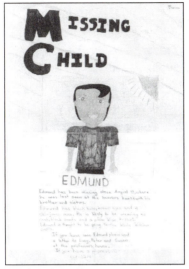

Maxine, Age 12

Character Profiles, Sketches and Posters

Students can hone their understanding of character relationships by producing character profiles, sketches and posters too. As readers work through a text, have them record what they learn about the different characters in jot notes or paragraphs. These descriptions can later be coupled with drawings or illustrations of the character. Information about a character may appear in the form of a biographical poster as well. While reading *The Lion, the Witch and the Wardrobe* and *The Castle in the Attic*, my students produced "missing persons" posters and reports featuring a physical description, the last known whereabouts and the possible destination of characters who disappeared in parts of the novel. Readers, then, examined the role that other characters played in their disappearance, search or recovery.

Questions

Sometimes the content of a novel is so compelling that it provokes readers to ask questions about the characters, setting or events in the story. A reading response log is a good place for students to keep a record of their questions. As they delve deeper into the text, readers may discover answers to the questions they raised and explain them in discussion groups or other written entries.

While reading the novel *The Castle in the Attic*, a student in my class posed questions to ten-year-old William, the main character, after he used a magic token to shrink his nanny, Mrs. Philips:

> *Don't you think you were selfish to do such a thing?*
> *Don't you think that someone will find out eventually?*
> *Are you proud of what you did?*
> *Why couldn't you just let Mrs. Philips go back to England?*
>
> *Charlene, Age 11*

Later, the reader examines the character's intentions and motives and addresses these questions in her next response entry:

> *William feels bad about what he did but I don't think he regrets it that much. Now he is more lonely even though he still has Mrs. Philips with him…*

"Meanwhile Back at the Ranch" Episodes

Another effective response technique presented in Kooy and Wells's book is a "Meanwhile back at the ranch" episode. In this strategy, students hypothesize about what is happening to characters "off-stage" using textual clues and later, record these assumptions in their reading response log. Writing about these unknown circumstances can help readers understand the connections among characters in a novel. While reading *The Castle in the Attic*, one student in my class wrote about the events happening back at William's home after the young boy shrunk himself and began his adventure with Sir Simon, the knight:

Meanwhile back at William's house, time is standing still. If time wasn't standing still, William's parents would be panicking because William was missing. They also would have been wondering why Mrs. Philips hadn't called when she got to England or before she left. Mrs. Lawrence would be losing sleep and Mr. Lawrence would be putting up posters of William as he searched the city for him.

Jessica, Age 11

Writing as Response

Writing about literature can be a powerful way for students to engage in response. Using this response mode requires students to write for a variety of purposes: to inform, convince, imagine, convey emotions and learn. The value of written responses to literature rests in the possibilities they offer learners to express their perspectives of a text in a variety of ways. Writing experiences may focus on basic elements of story, aspects of the chosen theme or the reader's subjective reactions to a text.

Responding to literature in various forms gives students a voice and adds style and enthusiasm to their writing. Response writing may take many forms, including:

- Journal entries;
- Writing-in-role;
- Letter writing;
- Newspaper reports and magazine articles;
- Predictions and forecasts;
- Story sequels and additional chapters;
- Alternative endings;
- Creative spin-offs;
- Documentaries;
- Critical reviews (e.g., book reviews);
- Creative writing (e.g., short stories, descriptive paragraphs, poetry)

Journal Entries
Readers can respond to novels by producing journal entries. Keeping a journal enables students to express their emotions and personal reactions to a book in writing. Journals may take different forms, including:

- Reading response journal;
- Literature/reading log;
- Dialogue journal.

A journal is a record of a reader's responses to a novel. Students can respond to literature in a variety of ways in their journals. Journal entries may include:

- Personal opinions and reactions to the story;
- Interpretations of story elements;
- Related life experiences;

Paul, Age 12

- Questions or issues for further thought or discussion;
- Predictions of upcoming events;
- Inferences and judgements of the text;
- Solutions to conflicts in the novel;
- Comments about the writing style;
- Suggestions for the author;
- Observations of the reading process.

Keeping a journal also allows students to share their responses with others, understand alternative viewpoints, and make both personal and collective meaning of a text. While reading a novel, learners may choose to share the content of their journal with others through discussion or in writing.

Writing-in-Role

Writing-in-role is a powerful way to engage readers in a text. This enriching writing and drama activity allows students to explore different viewpoints. In it, students imagine themselves to be a character in a literary work and write from that character's point of view. Readers can explore the emotions and actions of different characters by writing-in-role in diary or journal entries designated for this purpose. Writing from different points of view helps learners understand characters' feelings, intentions, dilemmas, behaviors and relationships with others. Writing-in-role can also deepen children's awareness and sensitivity to the world and make them empathetic, compassionate and considerate of the feelings of others.

This is best exemplified in the words of the following student who wrote a diary entry to describe Jesse's grief following Leslie's death in the novel *Bridge to Terabithia*:

> *Jesse was in a state of denial when he found out that Leslie died. You could tell that Jesse was so sad that he began to sort of feel mad:*
>
> *Dear Diary,*
>
> *Why did Leslie have to die? I don't know what I'm going to do. Leslie was a friend that I had deep in my heart. Now, I just have a memory of her that I might forget someday.*
> *Even though I am sad about Leslie, the sympathy that people are showing me is making me mad! I feel sad and hurt enough that Leslie died that I don't need people reminding me of her...I don't want so much sympathy.*
>
> *(Signed) Jesse*
>
> Jessica, Age 11

Here, the reader makes a strong connection with the character on an emotional level, revealing the depth of her understanding of this element of the story.

Letter Writing

Readers can respond to a text using a letter-writing strategy. Experiences in letter writing allow students to explore character relationships and story conflicts. Letter writing can take many forms. For example, children can write letters to characters in novels they have read. Through correspondence, readers can develop empathy, construct an understanding and establish a relationship with a character in a book. Learners can also recount story experiences, describe character relationships and explain plot developments by writing letters from one character to another.

Important issues in the text can be addressed in advice letters too. While reading the novel *The Belonging Place*, one student wrote a letter to an advice columnist seeking solutions to the main character's problems:

> *Dear Abby,*
>
> *My name is Elspet Mary. I am writing you this letter because I need some advice. My family wants to move to Upper Canada but I don't want to go because I will miss my friends, Glen Buchan and all the other things.*
>
> *I like living in Scotland. I don't want to move. My other problem is that we are going on a ship to Upper Canada. I am afraid because my real dad died at sea because of a storm and his ship broke down. I am scared that the same thing is going to happen to us when we go to Upper Canada and I am afraid that there might be a storm. I kind of want to go because I want to be with my family. What do I do?*
>
> *Sincerely,*
> *Elspet Mary*

> *Lavaniya, Age 9*

The student later offers solutions to these problems in a reply letter.

Newspaper Reports and Magazine Articles

Following a reading experience, students can respond to a novel by writing a newspaper report or magazine article about important elements in the story (e.g., events, theme etc.). While reading the novel *The Pinballs*, my students wrote articles for a teenage magazine that featured a special edition on foster homes and the important relationships that children can form being members of a foster family. Reworking a text in such a way challenges students to revisit a novel, examine content closely, make inferences, fill in missing details and respond to literature using another writing form.

Predictions and Forecasts

During a novel encounter, students can examine aspects of story by noting plot developments and making predictions of upcoming events in their writing. By revisiting these predictions, students can affirm or alter them to reflect events that have actually occurred in the story. Readers can forecast events that deal with character relationships and setting too.

While reading the novel *Sarah, Plain and Tall*, a fourth grader explains his predictions in writing. His written response provides insight about the main character, her relationship with others and the setting of the book:

> *I think that Sarah will be very happy when she comes to visit. I think that she will like the father and the children. I think she will feel happy about living on a farm. Sarah will teach the children how to sing. They will spend time together. Sarah will tell everyone about her life. I think Sarah will decide to stay in their house.*
>
> *Faraz, Age 9*

Story Sequels, Alternative Endings, Creative Spin-offs etc.
Response writing activities may lead to the formation or reconstruction of a new text. Following a novel experience, students can write an alternative ending, extend a story, write an additional chapter or sequel, modernize an old text or write an epilogue to the story. After reading *The Pinballs*, the students in my class wrote a sequel ten years after the children left the foster home to describe changes in their lives and their ongoing relationships with one another.

After reading a literary work, students can also write documentaries, critical reviews, letters to the author and creative spin-offs. Readers might expand on a text by writing a dialogue between two characters that can be included as part of a television or movie script.

Creative Writing
Response activities may even inspire students to write literature themselves. Creative writing experiences offer students the opportunity to develop their own writing style, to strengthen their voice as authors, and to use their reading responses to produce their own literary works.

Students may choose to write short stories and novels based on a prior reading experience. These works of literature may include the same characters or deal with similar topics, themes, conflicts or settings as in a novel they have read. After reading the novel *The Lion, the Witch and the Wardrobe* by C.S. Lewis, my students wrote other adventure stories that took place in Narnia. These adventures were based on character relationships in the original Narnia series.

Students can extend their responses to literature by creating works of poetry too. The content of a poem may deal with story elements in the novel or aspects of the chosen theme. One student in my class produced a character profile of the protagonist in the novel *Sarah, Plain and Tall* by writing the cinquain poem shown on this page.

Creating a poem about the main character in this novel helped the reader consolidate his understanding of the relationship the protagonist would have with the other characters in the book.

Sarah
Nice, beautiful
Helps, cleans, cooks
She likes to draw

Faraz, Age 9

Responding through the Arts

Experiences with literature can be enriched through arts activities too. Arts activities provide students with opportunities to use their imagination to respond to texts in different ways. Children's experiences with the arts have a magical way of releasing the imagination and giving it room to grow.

Responding to literature through visual arts, drama, dance, music and other creative activities allows students to have interactive and meaningful experiences inside works of literature. Learners are challenged to envision, extend, invent and use their imagination to produce works of art based on the experiences in a book. Readers are able to explore story elements and aspects of theme in an artistic way. These experiences allow young people to produce active, creative, emotional and authentic forms of response. As readers interact with a text, they can express themselves using a variety of art forms, including:

- Visual arts — story illustrations, water color paintings, paper mâché, drawings, collages, 3-D models, dioramas, murals;
- Music — song medleys, singing, writing lyrics, listening to music;
- Dance — improvisational dance, creative movement, choreography;
- Drama — mime, tableaux, improvisation, role-playing, scripted stories;
- Audiovisual — animation, special effects, film production;
- Other — photography.

Visual Arts

Aspects of novels can be depicted through visual arts experiences. Students can interpret elements of story and articulate their responses through illustrations and artwork of their own. In order to use this form of response effectively:

- Teach students how to use particular art techniques.
- Provide learners with a variety of supplies and materials that they can explore on their own.
- Examine illustrations in a variety of texts with the class and discuss the various artistic styles used by illustrators of children's books.
- Read aloud sections of a novel that include vivid descriptions or create powerful visual images.
- Challenge the students to express these images in different ways, including collages, paintings, charcoal drawings and other illustrative forms.

While reading the novel *Bridge to Terabithia*, my students produced pastel drawings of the kingdom of Terabithia, an imaginary place created by Leslie and Jesse as a symbol of their friendship. Readers can express their reactions to a text by producing abstract works of art that capture their emotional response in a unique way. Literary interpretations can be artistically presented in scrapbooks, dioramas and book cover designs too.

Bismattie & Lisa, Age 11

Paul, Age 12

Music and Dance

Experiences with novels can be enriched through music activities as well. Story elements (e.g., plot developments) can be retold through song. Students can select music or create their own compositions to accompany the scenes from a novel. After locating musical selections that deal with similar topics, issues or themes from a text, learners can compile them into a song medley. Readers can also create a sound track to accompany a novel they have read, listen to music that reflects character relationships or prepare choral performances to present to others.

Music activities can be accompanied by dance experiences too. Story events, character relationships, scene changes and other narrative elements can be interpreted through creative movement set to music. Students can compose dance sequences to demonstrate scenes from a novel, important events, interactions among characters and personal reactions to the story. After reading the novel *Bridge to Terabithia*, my students used music, costumes, props, dance elements (e.g., timing) and non-verbal strategies (e.g., gestures, facial expressions) to depict scenes like building the bridge, finding Terabithia, Leslie's death and other important story developments that impacted on the lives of the characters and their relationships.

Drama

Readers can also use drama to respond to novels. Dramatic experiences can extend students' understanding of literature by enabling them to examine story elements from different perspectives. The characters, themes, issues, settings and events of a novel can be explored in a variety of ways.

For example, students may wish to present parts of a novel through tableaux. A tableau is a frozen picture of a scene, idea or theme from a story. Students usually work in cooperative groups to select an event or concept and explore various ways it can be represented physically (e.g., using gestures, facial expressions etc.). Afterwards, the group presents its tableau to the class. A discussion usually follows on how the scene was depicted.

Improvisation is another interesting way to experience a novel. Improvisational drama or role-playing is not scripted or rehearsed. The drama world is created, developed and sustained by participants talking, listening and responding in role. Students can role-play a scene from a novel or another imaginative situation (e.g., a chance encounter between two characters) based on a book. Story props, costumes or puppets can also be used to re-enact or improvise events from novels.

Setting up an inquiry about the conflicts or events of a story is another engaging drama experience. Readers disclose issues, problems and experiences by assuming the role of a character in a novel (including marginalized characters) or a member of the surrounding community. As part of the inquiry, members of the community are called together to participate in a town meeting, a trial or other public gathering to uncover untold events and details in order to bring justice. While reading the novel *The Castle in the Attic*, the students in my class conducted a court trial to determine the fate of Alastor, the evil wizard, following his acts of cruelty. By assuming the role of witnesses, jurors and lawyers at his trial, learners were called upon to either defend, prosecute or explain their relationship to Alastor in the context of story events.

Interviewing is another response strategy that can be implemented as a drama experience. By assuming the roles of characters from novels and news reporters, students can interview one another in role about story conflicts, plot developments and themes. While reading *Bridge to Terabithia*, my students assumed the roles of Leslie, Jesse and a magazine reporter and conducted an interview about the special friendship the two characters developed in the story. The interview strategy can be used in news conferences, television and radio talk shows and other drama experiences where students have a forum to discuss controversial issues, moral dilemmas, character relationships and other story elements in role.

Students can also enjoy presenting a novel through read-aloud experiences such as choral performance. Various methods can be used to arrange a text for choral reading. A work of literature can be read in unison, two-part arrangements, line-by-line by different readers or accompanied by movement, sound effects or music. Changes in voice, tempo or volume can create different interpretations of the text. Parts of a book may be read aloud in sequence. Learners can use a range of techniques to add enthusiasm and appeal to the read-aloud event, including:

- Eye contact;
- Expressive voice;
- Visual aids (pictures, illustrations, props, symbols);
- Facial expressions;
- Background scenery;
- Special effects;
- Music;
- Lighting.

In reader's theatre, another form of read-aloud drama, students select a text to perform for others and practise reading it aloud. Readers then stage a literary work simply for the class. Props, music, costumes, sets and movement are not required. Meaning is conveyed through the use of voice only. Parts of a novel (e.g., chapter) can be scripted for reader's theatre. Individual readers assume the parts of different characters, create dialogue scripts and practise reading the speaking parts aloud. Narrator parts can be shared by several students. Participants practise reading their scripts aloud several times before performing for others. Roles can later be rotated. Audience performance does not have to be the intended goal.

Experiences with novels can lead to a number of other drama activities, including:

- Monologues;
- Storytelling;
- Puppet theatre;

- Plays;
- Scripted story writing and performance.

Audiovisual Productions

Students can explore narrative elements of a novel by viewing and/or creating audiovisual productions like films or screenplays. A motion picture can motivate students to read a book, help them understand a complex plot, provide a different perspective on the events or characters and/or stimulate a literary discussion. After reading the novel *The Pinballs*, my students watched a movie based on the book. In a follow-up discussion, learners compared the narrative elements, character relationships and other components of the novel and film.

A film can even be studied as an artform in itself. Viewers can examine features such as sound and lighting, special effects and other production components. Later, students can produce their own films or videos as a form of literary response. There are a number of steps involved in this process as shown in the margin.

A film production can involve members of the entire class as students work together behind the scenes and in front of the camera to reconstruct the novel into another artform. With assistance from the board's media services department, learners can create a successful production for others to see.

Other Response Formats

After responding to novels in discussion groups, reading response logs, writing and arts activities, readers can extend their experiences with literature in other ways. For example, students may wish to express their understanding of story elements and explore aspects of the chosen theme through graphic forms of response. Using a variety of non-verbal, illustrative and symbolic techniques, readers can produce:

- Maps (e.g., story map);
- Webs;
- Labelled diagrams;
- Column charts (e.g., compare and contrast, advantages and disadvantages);
- Lists;
- T-tables;
- Schedules/timetables;
- Advertisements and posters;
- Graphs.

These experiences require a close re-reading of the text. As students organize content using different formats they learn to analyze reading material, synthesize information and present literary details in a variety of graphic forms. Producing a variety of responses to literature using graphic forms, such as the one depicted on this page, enhances students' understanding of story elements and aspects of the theme.

Steps in Film/Video Production

1. Select a text to be videotaped.
2. Write the scripts (dialogue and shooting scripts).
3. Choose a location.
4. Select cast members.
5. Practise speaking parts.
6. Gather and make props and scenery.
7. Rehearse scenes.
8. Film the video/movie.
9. Edit the video.

Chores in Pioneer Times

Lavaniya, Age 10

Novel Exhibition and Museum Collection Display

Once students have read various novels in the collection and engaged in a variety of response activities, encourage them to share their accomplishments with others. As a class, plan a Novel Exhibition and Museum Collection Display.

Prior to the celebration, have students select projects, organize displays, practise oral presentations, rehearse dramatic performances and arrange demonstrations for the exhibition/museum. The event should showcase a collection of novels organized around a common theme, such as Relationships, along with work produced by the students themselves. Arrangements should be made to hold the exhibits in different parts of the school. Oral presentations (e.g., choral readings, panel discussions etc.) and drama/dance performances may be held in the gymnasium, auditorium or library. Artwork, writing samples and media projects may be featured in classrooms, display cases and along the corridors. Advertisements and posters that highlight the main features of the exhibition/museum can be made to broadcast the event. Students can design programs outlining exhibit locations, presentation outlines and performance times for the events. Invitations can be extended to various guests, including children's book authors, parents, administrators, teachers, students and community members.

During the tour, visitors can fill in passports marking the exhibits they attend and record personal commentaries and reviews of the work displayed. Following the Novel Exhibition and Museum Collection Display, students can be honored for their contributions in a gala presentation. Learners may attend this part of the celebration dressed as characters in novels they read. At the final gala, readers can share their personal reactions, feelings and responses to the literature activities in which they engaged.

EXTENSION ACTIVITIES

Encounters with novels can be extended in a variety of ways that may enrich the literature experience. As readers participate in a novel program they can:

- Read and respond to novels of a similar genre (e.g., historical, fantasy, science fiction) or by the same author (e.g., Katherine Patterson, Eleanor Coerr).
- Produce newspapers, magazines and other forms of media (e.g., commercials) based on novels in the theme collection.
- Create multimedia projects (e.g., design Web sites) based on novels.
- Invite children's authors to the school to discuss novels they have written.
- Visit publishers of children's literature to learn about how novels are produced.

- Read novels aloud to community members in seniors' homes, hospitals, local libraries etc. and produce responses together.
- Compose novel text sets of their own based on topics of interest.
- Use response strategies to explore short stories, picture books, poems, plays, myths, fables, fairy tales and other works of children's literature related to the same theme.
- Read and respond to novels that deal with a variety of topics and themes, such as:
  - universal issues (e.g., war, peace, freedom);
  - generic concepts (e.g., fantasy, magic);
  - social conditions (e.g., relationships, justice);
  - human needs (e.g., health, self-esteem, spirituality);
  - environmental topics (e.g., animal protection, resource conservation);
  - historical periods (e.g., Middle Ages, Pioneer Times).
- Engage in multidisciplinary activities based on the experiences in a novel. Story conflicts, character relationships, settings, theme aspects and other narrative elements can be explored through related topics and learning experiences in different subject areas, as illustrated on the following page.

Readers of all ages enjoy the enticing quality of a good book. Children and adults alike are intrigued by the profound storylines, memorable characters, vivid settings and compelling themes that a novel can provide. A growing number of teachers are integrating novels into all curriculum areas in elementary-level classrooms and devising learning activities that will enhance children's experiences with literature.

Using a response-based approach, young readers can interact with a text and construct meaning in a variety of ways. A number of engagement strategies have been presented in this chapter, including discussion, reading response, writing and arts activities. There are an endless number of other ways that readers can interact with a text. Whatever the techniques may be, response modes should include authentic experiences with literature.

Reading and responding to novels facilitates the building of knowledge and language skills in an intricate way. Apart from understanding the characteristics of the genre, elements of story and various themes, readers will develop higher-level processes such as critical and creative thinking.

In a novel program, reading should be a memorable, worthwhile and personal experience. Encounters with literature should provide opportunities for creative, reflective and active expressions of response that will enable readers to construct meaning. Personal involvement in the story world will lead to greater understanding of literary texts and life itself.

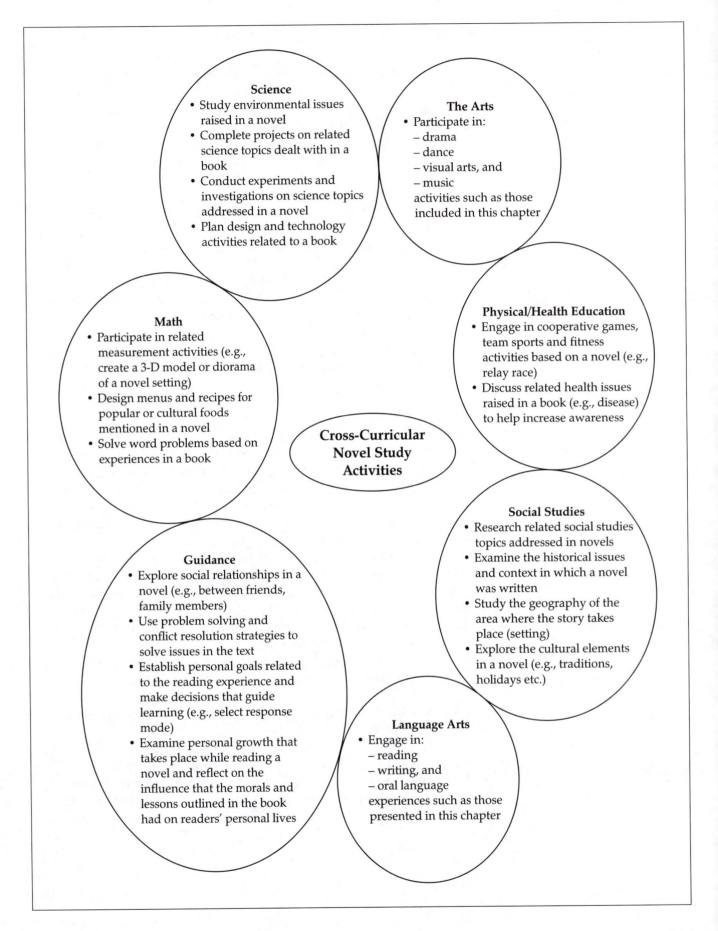

Science
- Study environmental issues raised in a novel
- Complete projects on related science topics dealt with in a book
- Conduct experiments and investigations on science topics addressed in a novel
- Plan design and technology activities related to a book

The Arts
- Participate in:
  - drama
  - dance
  - visual arts, and
  - music
  activities such as those included in this chapter

Math
- Participate in related measurement activities (e.g., create a 3-D model or diorama of a novel setting)
- Design menus and recipes for popular or cultural foods mentioned in a novel
- Solve word problems based on experiences in a book

Physical/Health Education
- Engage in cooperative games, team sports and fitness activities based on a novel (e.g., relay race)
- Discuss related health issues raised in a book (e.g., disease) to help increase awareness

Cross-Curricular Novel Study Activities

Guidance
- Explore social relationships in a novel (e.g., between friends, family members)
- Use problem solving and conflict resolution strategies to solve issues in the text
- Establish personal goals related to the reading experience and make decisions that guide learning (e.g., select response mode)
- Examine personal growth that takes place while reading a novel and reflect on the influence that the morals and lessons outlined in the book had on readers' personal lives

Social Studies
- Research related social studies topics addressed in novels
- Examine the historical issues and context in which a novel was written
- Study the geography of the area where the story takes place (setting)
- Explore the cultural elements in a novel (e.g., traditions, holidays etc.)

Language Arts
- Engage in:
  - reading
  - writing, and
  - oral language
  experiences such as those presented in this chapter

CHAPTER TWO

Publishing Picture Books

Visual stories that concentrate on story development and interdependence

From a young age, children are fascinated with picture books and the delightful language, creative illustrations and entertaining stories they provide. More and more students in elementary schools today are encountering picture books in their primary-, junior- and intermediate-level classrooms. Regardless of age, picture books offer something for everyone.

Picture books can nourish a love for language, a fascination with stories, an interest in pictures, and an enjoyment for reading and writing. A picture book unit organized around a particular topic or theme, such as Interdependence, enables students to build knowledge and language skills in an integrated way. Young readers can learn the characteristics of the genre, the techniques authors use to construct story elements and strategies that can be applied to the publication of their own picture book, all within a thematic framework.

INTRODUCING THE GENRE/THEME

Using Picture Books to Teach the Elements of Writing

Picture books comprise a rich literary genre that offers enjoyment to children and adults of all ages. The enchanting quality of the words and illustrations often captivate readers, young and old alike. In this genre, the talents and styles of both an author and illustrator are brought together to produce a work of fiction.

Placing picture books at the centre of the language curriculum can enhance the reading and writing connection. As readers interact with such literature, they engage with authors in ways that can inspire them to produce their own works of fiction. Picture books, like other narratives, provide young people with models for their own writing. Trade books and children's literature collections organized around a particular theme can be used as tools to teach children the writer's craft. Examining the techniques authors use to compose literary elements can serve as frameworks for students when writing and publishing their own picture books.

When children are taught to write like authors, the creative powers of their imagination begin to unfold in remarkable ways. Suddenly they are capable of producing works of fiction that are filled with elements of magic, wonder, sentiment or realism. Each word and picture on the page brings the characters and stories to life.

Creating Theme-Related Picture Book Text Sets

The endless number of picture books available today offers a wide selection of literature for teachers to draw from as they develop text sets built around common themes or curriculum areas. A text set can be constructed by selecting a number of high-quality picture books filled with expressive language, exemplary illustrations, creative ideas, diverse writing styles and a variety of reading levels that reflect students' different abilities. A book list of titles and authors related to a particular theme can then be developed as a basis for a genre study such as the one presented in this chapter.

The concept of Interdependence is a fascinating theme to explore through picture books. In a world of diversity, conflict and change, it is important for students to understand that humans remain closely connected through communication systems, information networks, and common goals and experiences. By sharing information, resources and efforts, communities from around the globe can come together to build a stronghold for peace and safeguards for the environment. Cooperating with one another helps people make connections and appreciate their similarities and differences.

The notion of Interdependence affects us all in our family lives, friendships, local neighborhoods and wider global community. Picture books that deal with aspects of the theme of Interdependence, such as those listed at the end of the book, can communicate important messages to children of all ages. A picture book unit can also be organized around a variety of other appropriate themes.

After developing a thematic text set, encourage children to add to the collection with selections of their own. If possible, include multiple copies of some picture books within the collection. Finally, select books from the text set that can be used to teach literary elements such as setting, characters, beginnings, endings, time and other aspects of story writing effectively.

KNOWLEDGE/SKILL COMPONENTS

Studying and publishing picture books allows young people to build knowledge and language skills in a meaningful and authentic way. Exploring and creating narratives through a variety of learning experiences, such as those presented in this chapter, enables students to:

- Understand the characteristics of picture books;
- Identify the elements of story;
- Explore a variety of writing styles, skills and techniques used by children's authors and illustrators;
- Identify characteristics of quality literature that can be used as writing models;

- Examine picture books in text set collections and respond to literature in a variety of ways (e.g., in writing, through discussion etc.);
- Read and write for a variety of purposes;
- Use various strategies to make sense of texts and analyze elements of story;
- Write picture books, incorporating the features of narratives (setting, characters, plot, theme) and other aspects of stories (e.g., dialogue) into their work;
- Use their imagination and draw on life experiences to describe settings, create characters, construct plots, write dialogue and build themes for their stories;
- Apply a variety of writing strategies to develop different parts of the narrative (e.g., effective beginnings and endings);
- Use their knowledge of the organization, structure and features of a picture book to publish their own book;
- Work independently and collaboratively through the stages of the writing process;
- Use a variety of art techniques and materials to create illustrations for their picture books.

The learning activities in this chapter are designed to help students discover the particular characteristics of picture books related to a chosen theme, such as Interdependence. Learners will investigate different components of writing a story, explore a variety of writing skills and techniques, and later, apply knowledge of story elements and language conventions to their own writing. The teaching strategies provided will guide students through the stages of the writing process as they publish their own picture books. Students will later plan a learning celebration where their picture books can be shared with others at a Publisher's Fair and Literary Awards Presentation.

INTRODUCTORY ACTIVITIES

Exploring Picture Book Text Sets

To introduce the genre, share the collection of picture books organized around a common theme that you have gathered with the class. Read several books in the text set aloud. Invite learners to respond in a response journal or reading response log. Provide an opportunity for students to read, explore, discuss and respond to picture books in the thematic collection individually, in pairs or in small groups. Ask learners to keep a list of picture books they have read.

As a class, hold book talks and reading conferences to discuss picture books in the collection through the sharing of personal interpretations and related experiences. Ask students to identify the characters, settings, plots, themes and other story elements (e.g., conflicts) in the picture books and make general comparisons. Once the children have had an opportunity to explore the text set in these ways, they can begin examining the characteristics of this genre more fully.

Identifying the Features of a Picture Book

Encourage the students to review the picture books in the text set collection. Ask them to identify common elements or features included in these works of fiction. Have readers examine the format, layout and parts of the picture books closely. As a class, brainstorm the common components of picture books and produce a reference list. This list might look like the one shown here.

Later, the students should try to include these features in their own picture books. The list can be used as a guide during the publication process.

> **Features of a Picture Book**
>
> - Cover
> - Endpapers
> - Inside title page
> - Dedication page
> - Text (body)
> - Illustrations
> - Author profile
> - Plot summary
> - Book reviews and commentaries
> - Book jacket

Examining Illustrations in Picture Books

Illustrations are an important feature in picture books. These visual images can captivate readers, transcend the page and bring a book to life. In groups, have students examine the content of picture book illustrations in the text set collection and produce a list that might include:

- The different settings in a book (e.g., landscapes, seascapes etc.);
- Character portraits;
- Story scenes;
- Important symbols.

Afterwards, ask students to examine the work of various illustrators and identify the variety of art materials and techniques used to produce the illustrations, for example:

- Paintings (watercolors, oil, acrylic etc.);
- Drawings (pastel, chalk, charcoal, pen and ink etc.);
- Sketches;
- Photographs (black and white, color etc.);
- 3-D models (plasticine, pop-up etc.);
- Border patterns and designs;
- Murals and collages.

In order for students to further understand the important function of illustrations, invite them to examine the pages of a wordless picture book and explain how pictures, themselves, can tell a story.

CORE ACTIVITIES

Deconstructing Texts

Picture books can serve as models for students' own writing. By examining the content of various picture books, young people can explore the range of writing skills and techniques that authors use to construct different narrative elements in their work. In the activities that follow, learners will have an opportunity to investigate the various components of a story and different writing strategies before creating their own picture books. Many of the learning experiences in this section are based on Ralph Fletcher's book *What a Writer Needs* and *Craft Lessons: Teaching Writing K-8*, by Ralph Fletcher and Joann Portalupi. The practical strategies and literary techniques they provide serve as springboards for lessons that can challenge, extend and develop students' writing.

Creating a Setting

The setting describes the world in which the characters live. It marks a place where the events of the story unfold. A setting is often a good starting point for a story.

In order to help students develop a sense of setting, read a picture book from the thematic collection that effectively portrays this story element to the class. Later, discuss the various scenes and places in the story. Encourage the students to reread parts of the book and select key phrases used by the author to describe the different settings in the picture book. As a class, examine the vocabulary and literary devices used to create vivid images of settings.

While examining this story element with my class, I read a picture book from the Interdependence text set collection entitled *The Crane Girl* by Veronica Martenova Charles, a story that explores the interdependence of family, nature and cultural tradition. After making a list of the various settings described in the book (e.g., village, beach, forest, hilltop, garden etc.), the students and I examined the way adjectives were effectively used to create imagery (e.g., rippling water, sunlit branches).

Through the use of guided imagery and visualization, invite the children to close their eyes and envision a place (real or imaginary). In order to develop their sensory awareness, ask probing questions like:

- What does this place look like?
- What does it smell like?
- What sounds do you hear?
- What does it feel like? Is there anything you can touch?
- If you could taste it, what would it taste like?

In order to develop a main setting for their own picture book, have the students record images, thoughts and ideas about the place they just imagined using their senses, as shown on the handout featured on the following page. Next, encourage learners to use literary devices (e.g., similes, metaphors) to describe their setting in detail.

Paul, Age 11

Creating a Setting

Select a setting for your story (real or imaginary).
Use your senses to explain this place.
Create similes and metaphors that describe the scene(s).
Record your thoughts in the spaces below.

TOUCH: _____

_____

SMELL: _____

_____

SIGHT: _____

_____

SOUND: _____

_____

TASTE: _____

_____

_____

Organize your thoughts and ideas into sentences and write a paragraph describing the setting you just created.

_____

_____

_____

_____

_____

_____

_____

_____

_____

Include this description as part of your picture book.

Following this activity, my students were able to describe settings in their own picture books using vivid word choices and powerful images that enabled the reader to envision the scenes in the story:

> As I touched the soft sand near the beach, I could smell the fresh misty salt water. I could see the pretty pebbles beneath the waves and I heard a flock of dancing birds fly by. Then I tasted the rippling water. It was cool and refreshing.
>
> *Jagjeet, Age 10*

> In the valley where the sun was bright and the air was sweet stood a cabin. Beside the cabin was a stream. The water sparkled in the sunlight and tasted fresh and sweet. You could hear the singing of the birds and the soft whispers of the wind. The peaceful sounds, smells and sights of the valley surrounded the cabin. The ground was as soft as a pillow you could sleep on. The water passed under the trees and moved over the rocks like the turning pages of a book.
>
> *Sheriza, Age 12*

Creating a Character

Young writers need help developing characters that come to life. As readers, they must understand different literary elements, including aspects of a character's public life and private image. As writers, they should be aware of the importance of creating a healthy balance between these two crucial elements when developing characters of their own.

As a class, begin by reviewing the various aspects of character by revisiting the activities presented in the novel chapter, where students explored this story element in detail. Next, introduce students to different strategies and literary techniques that can be used to develop and describe a character in a piece of writing.

For example, to help students create a main character for their own picture book, have them do the following:

- Picture the character in their mind.
- Imagine a conversation that might take place with the character during a first encounter.
- Pretend that they have just read a personal entry in the character's diary/journal.
- Describe aspects of the character's public and private lives to a partner.
- Select particular features they wish to share about the character (e.g., physical appearance, habits, interests etc.).
- Choose a narrative technique (first or third person) to describe their character.

Mohammad, Age 11

Ideas can be recorded on a handout like the one shown on the opposite page.

This young writer brings her character to life in a way that enables readers to picture the character, get to know her and understand the role she might play in her community:

> *Marium is from Jerusalem. She is a very kind and patient person. Her hair is silky and long. Her walk is graceful. Marium is not poor and she is not rich. Her voice sounds beautiful like a nightingale. When she speaks, her voice is soft and comforting. Marium is cheerful and sensitive. She is not a stranger to people in her village.*
>
> Sheriza, Age 12

Writing Effective Beginnings

A well-crafted beginning is the best way to start a piece of writing. An effective lead has the power to entice readers and interest them in a story. Over the years, I have noticed that young writers often begin narratives with overused phrases like "Once upon a time…", "Long ago…"or "There once was…" as a way of inviting readers into a text. Children as authors need to be taught that there are more effective ways of beginning a work of fiction.

In order to demonstrate the power of an intriguing lead, select several picture books from the text set collection that begin with an effective opening line, sentence or paragraph, and read them aloud to the class. Following each one, discuss the introduction to the book and examine the ways in which the author's word choices and writing style result in a well-crafted story beginning.

In my class, I read the opening paragraph of several picture books from the Interdependence text set collection to my students, including *The Perfect Crane* and *A Time for Toys*. These books demonstrate the important role of interdependence in fostering friendship, hope and survival among people. Their well-crafted story beginnings also provide interesting models for students' own writing.

After sharing examples of various leads from different literary works, have the students recall some of their favorite stories and explain what made the beginning of the book interesting and motivating to read. As a class, discuss the criteria for good beginnings and produce a list of qualities for effective leads. These might include:

- Descriptive language that introduces the setting or main character;
- Interesting details about the plot;
- Surprising facts or shocking information;
- Clues about the story conflict;
- A glimpse of the ending;
- A sense of wonder, mystery or adventure that intrigues readers;
- A question that invites readers into the story;
- A glance into a story scene or conversation among the characters.

Premal, Age 11

Ajay, Age 11

CREATING A CHARACTER

Create a character for your picture book.
Describe the person in detail.
Record your thoughts below.

Name of Character: _____

Physical Appearance:_____

_____

Personal Background: _____

_____

Accomplishments: _____

_____

Emotions (Feelings):_____

_____

Inner Thoughts: _____

_____

Conflicts/Problems: _____

_____

Interests: _____

_____

Fears: _____

_____

Gestures and Motions:_____

_____

Habits: _____

_____

Other: _____

_____

Organize your thoughts and ideas into sentences and write a paragraph describing the character you just created.

_____

_____

_____

_____

_____

_____

_____

After discussing strategies for writing effective beginnings, provide students with an opportunity to review the thematic picture books in the text set collection. In groups, ask the children to locate examples of various leads and make a list of effective story beginnings from reading material.

Encourage students to apply these various strategies to their own writing and use a different type of lead for each story they write. The young writers featured on this page explored different options while developing the introductions to their picture books dealing with aspects of Interdependence.

Writing Effective Endings

The ending of a story is one of the most important parts of a narrative and the part that often lingers in the reader's mind and makes them feel satisfied or uneasy about a piece of writing they have just read. Young writers often struggle with ways to end a work of fiction, frequently choosing an abrupt ending or unresolved conclusion encompassing the phrase "… and they lived happily ever after" or "The End."

In order to help students write effective endings to their narratives, select picture books from the text set collection that have well-crafted story endings and read them aloud to the class. In my classroom, I read the story ending of *Sadako* by Eleanor Coerr and other Interdependence-related picture books that demonstrated to the students both the power of a strong conclusion and the importance of interdependence in upholding world peace. After such a presentation, ask students to find examples from picture books they have read that had memorable conclusions. As a class, produce a list of criteria for effective story endings. An effective story ending may:

- Provide solutions to the story conflict(s);
- Explain the fate of the characters;
- Have surprising or shocking elements;
- Appeal to the reader's emotions (make the reader feel happy or sad);
- Be withheld and leave the reader guessing;
- Return back to the beginning of the story after explaining a series of events;
- Offer a memorable conclusion that has a lasting impression on the reader.

Provide the children with an opportunity to review the picture books in the text set collection. In groups, ask learners to produce a list of effective story endings in the theme books. Later, compare the story endings and discuss their effectiveness as a class. Finally, encourage the students to use different types of endings in their own picture books. The young writers featured on this page wrote endings that left a lasting impression on the reader about the importance of Interdependence long after the story was over.

Using Dialogue

A well-crafted picture book is an elegant tool for teaching the art of writing and the development of characters, setting and other narrative elements. It is also a great place to begin an exploration of how dialogue can enhance a story. Using sophisticated tools like spoken dialogue can help young writers refine a story, develop character relationships, improve language usage and incorporate a natural form of communication into their work.

Before using discourse in their own writing, young authors should examine the use of dialogue in children's literature. To do this, select picture books from the thematic collection that include discussions among characters. Share examples of these literary conversations with the class by reading them aloud. Afterwards, discuss the content of each discourse and its role in the narrative. Produce a list of criteria for the effective use of dialogue in stories. This might include:

- Vibrant and active language;
- Content that is relevant to the story;
- Important information that contributes to the development of the narrative (e.g., reveals unknown details about the characters, plot etc.);
- Appropriate use of voice and suitable vocabulary for the character(s) involved in the conversation;
- Language that sounds authentic and is filled with nuances of human speech (e.g., interruptions, sighs, grammatical errors, sentence fragments etc.).

Next, invite students to select picture books in the text set that contain interesting dialogues among the characters. Using reader's theatre, have learners re-enact these literary conversations in groups. In order to help students generate dialogue for their own picture books, you may wish to provide them with a variety of other pre-writing activities. For example:

- Ask students to select characters from a book they have read and role-play a conversation between them.
- Have learners construct a comic strip depicting their favorite literary, television or movie characters using talk bubbles or dialogue balloons.

As young authors begin to use spoken dialogue in their writing, they are faced with the challenge of using quotation marks correctly. In fact, many students begin to experiment with this form of punctuation on their own. In dealing with this technical skill, you may wish to:

- Review with the class the parts of a picture book that contain dialogues among the characters.
- Examine the use of quotation marks closely, noting the format, structure and forms of punctuation used in literary conversations.
- Construct a list of rules for the use of quotation marks in direct speech. These may include:
  – Begin a new paragraph for each speaker and indent the first word.

Bismattie, Age 11

– Capitalize the first letter within an opening quotation mark.
– Keep most punctuation marks (e.g., commas, question marks) within the quotation marks.

To write effective dialogue it is also important to vary the verbs describing the action of speaking. As a class, produce a list of words, such as the ones shown on this page, that authors can use in place of the word *said* when writing story dialogue. By referring to the picture books in the text set collection, a thesaurus and other writing resources, have the students develop reference lists of their own for the word *said* that can be used when writing dialogues and conversations in their own stories.

> **Other Words for *Said***
> • explained
> • mentioned
> • asked
> • exclaimed
> • pronounced
> • expressed
> • asked
> • replied
> • answered

Marking the Passage of Time

There are many ways that writers make transitions from one point in time to another in a work of fiction. Skilled writers use a range of literary tools to mark the passage of time in their narratives. Young authors need help handling the complex element of time in their writing, to avoid such an overused phrase as "and then…" being repeated throughout a piece of writing.

In order to help students handle linear time and explain events chronologically in their work, select several picture books from the thematic collection that demonstrate the passage of time in an effective way and read them aloud to the class. Next, discuss the element of time in the stories and produce a list of transition words and phrases that authors use to mark the passage of time effectively. These might include:

• Early that morning…
• In the late afternoon…
• Later that night…
• The next day…
• The following evening…
• Suddenly…
• Soon after…

Afterwards, provide the students with an opportunity to review the picture books in the thematic collection in groups and locate additional words or phrases that authors use to show the passage of time in children's literature. Encourage readers to record examples of transition words and phrases on chart paper for future reference.

To reinforce the concept, provide students with opportunities to use sequence words and phrases in a variety of activities. For example:

• Ask the children to select the five main events in a picture book and summarize them in a paragraph using connecting words like *first, then, next, after* and *finally* at the beginning of each sentence.
• Have groups of students create a series of tableaux to depict the most important events in a picture book they have read and mark the beginning of each frozen picture using large note cards that have transition words written on them.
• Encourage students to use different language connectors (e.g., The next day…, Later that night…, Soon after… etc.), complex phrases

Lavaniya, Age 11

Ever since their country was invaded by King Sarin and his army, the nation was divided. The evil King Sarin had divided the country so that King Sarin's people would have the beautiful things and king Cranchi's people would be left to die if they did not work for King Sarin.

Many people did not work for King Sarin because they heard of all the evil things he had done. No one wanted to be under his rule.

A long time ago King Cranchi was the ruler of their country. That was when their country was beautiful. No one was out on the street, there was no sickness, and everyone was living the good life until the invasion.

Charlene, Age 11

and descriptive words to demonstrate sequence in their own writing.

Through the use of transition words, language connectors and other sequence strategies, young writers can begin to handle time in sophisticated ways that add charm and style to their writing.

Building Themes

The theme is an important aspect of a story that communicates a message or lesson to the reader. The main topic, subject, issue or problem in a work of literature is often related to the theme. Young authors may find the task of developing a theme for their picture book a challenging endeavor. Most experienced authors find that the theme develops as the story does.

Before developing a theme for their writing, students should be able to identify the main idea(s) in a work of literature. To do this, have learners examine picture books in the text set collection in groups and determine the following:

- The main subject or topic of different literary works (sometimes this may be revealed in the title);
- The problems, issues or conflicts in various stories;
- The moral lessons or messages in texts.

As a class, brainstorm aspects of the overall theme in the text set collection and produce a word web or concept map, such as the one shown here for Interdependence.

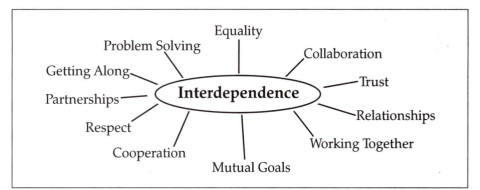

Once students are able to identify the main idea(s) in different works of fiction, they may begin to apply universal themes and topics to their own narrative writing. In order to apply theme aspects to the writing of their picture books, have students consider the subject, topic, problem, issue, lesson or message they want to communicate in their story and record ideas using a graphic organizer like the one shown.

Encourage young writers to select a concept related to the overall theme and develop story elements in a way that connects the theme components together. My students were able to build on theme aspects related to Interdependence (e.g., ideas of cooperation and problem solving) while writing their picture books. After describing the realities of war and poverty in many of their stories, these young writers developed strong characters whose cooperative efforts and problem-solving skills led to peaceful resolutions. Selecting a focus for their theme will guide students in their writing and add a new dimension to their story.

Using the Writing Process to Create a Picture Book

In order to prepare and publish their own picture books, introduce students to the steps of the writing process as outlined below. Assist them through the various stages of writing and publishing by providing pertinent strategies for each part of the process. It may help to revisit the lessons on story development in the previous section for effective techniques that can be applied to their own writing.

Pre-Writing Activities

Choosing a Theme-Related Topic
Begin by having students select a topic for their picture book. Ask them to review the content of picture books in the text set collection and re-examine aspects of the designated theme. In groups, ask students to generate a list of theme-related topics for their own writing. Encourage children to work with others to develop ideas for their stories. Sharing ideas with peers will help young writers discover the topics that readers are interested in. After selecting a topic for their story, students can plan other aspects of their picture book.

Selecting a Format
Before starting their writing, young authors need to select a format. As a class, review the characteristics of picture books in the text set collection and ask students to identify the features of different types of narratives. By applying their knowledge of the organization, structure and particular qualities of picture books to their work, students will be able to incorporate elements of story effectively into their own writing. Younger children should be encouraged to use the narrative form only in their picture books, while older students can be challenged to use other formats too (e.g., letter, journal, note, map, newspaper report etc.).

Choosing an Audience
After selecting a format for their writing, young authors need to decide on an audience for their story. Have students select an audience for their picture book by first generating a list of possible readers. These might include:

- Younger children;
- Adults (e.g., teacher, parents etc.);
- Peers;
- Family members;
- Other classes;
- Groups in the community (e.g., seniors).

It is important for students to decide on the intended audience prior to writing since this will influence the content and vocabulary they use in their picture book.

Deciding on a Purpose
The final decision that students should make prior to writing their picture book involves selecting a purpose for their story. Young authors should consider the theme, topic, format and audience of their book when deciding on a purpose for their writing. Generate a list of reasons why authors publish picture books to help students decide on a purpose. Writers of children's literature may want their stories to:

- Entertain readers;
- Raise issues;
- Explain events;
- Inform audiences;
- Teach moral lessons;
- Convey universal messages.

Preparing a Story Grammar

After making important decisions that will influence their writing, students are ready to gather and organize ideas for their picture book.

As part of the writing process, young writers are encouraged to gather information from a variety of sources and brainstorm ideas before writing a first draft. One format that can be introduced to students for recording thoughts and ideas related to a piece of writing is a story grammar.

Once students have selected a topic for their picture book related to the overall theme, have them generate ideas and outline each story element using the writing strategies taught previously. Encourage students to apply different techniques for developing characters, describing settings, constructing effective leads and composing other literary elements. Have students record their ideas in the different sections of a story grammar, such as in the ones illustrated here. This visual organizer helps the children develop aspects of the narrative before writing a first draft.

Writing a First Draft

Writing the first draft of a picture book involves organizing ideas in a story framework in order that it makes sense to the reader. Have students begin by writing a rough copy of the story itself. By referring to the notes outlined in their story grammar, young authors can produce a first draft either on the computer or on paper. Once students have written the story, have them work on the other components of their picture book too. In addition to writing a narrative, learners will need to write dedication pages, plot summaries for book covers and author profiles.

At this stage in the writing process, children do not need to be overly concerned about spelling, punctuation, grammar and other language

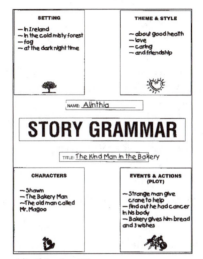

Alinthia, Age 10

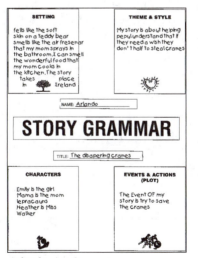

Arlando, Age 9

Adapted from the *First Steps Reading Resource Book* (Education Department of Western Australia, 1994)

conventions. The focus should primarily be on recording ideas in an interesting way that will later be revised and rewritten.

Revising and Rewriting

During the revision stage, the author makes sure that the content of the picture book is organized and written in a clear and logical way. Improvements can be made to the story by:

- Adding missing information;
- Leaving out unnecessary details;
- Changing the language where needed;
- Replacing ideas as needed;
- Moving around sentences/sections of text for better clarity.

In order to assist students with this stage, it may be necessary to use the overhead projector or chart paper to demonstrate different revision strategies. After selecting a sample text, show young writers how to eliminate unnecessary words and phrases or move sections of text in order to organize the story more effectively (e.g., cut and paste).

Encourage students to read their first draft aloud several times and focus on different components of their writing each time. Young writers should concentrate on the following elements:

- General content (e.g., clarity of ideas and information);
- Specific story elements (e.g., character profiles, descriptions of settings, beginnings, endings etc.);
- Organization (e.g., logical flow of ideas and sections);
- Language (e.g., variety of paragraphs, sentences, vocabulary, sequence words, dialogue).

After making necessary changes on their own, students can hold peer conferences with others as they continue to revise their work. Having other children review the content of their picture book can often strengthen students' writing. At the end of the revision process, learners should produce a second draft of their picture book that includes important changes and improvements in their writing.

Editing and Proofreading

After revising their picture book for content, flow of ideas and language usage, young authors should focus on the mechanics of writing by editing and proofreading their work for:

- Grammar;
- Punctuation;
- Spelling;
- Capitalization;
- Sentence structure;
- Other language conventions (e.g., writing style).

Students should focus on one aspect at a time during the editing process. At this stage, specific language skills may need to be taught in mini-lessons to help children improve their writing. Learners can use editing symbols to indicate changes that need to be made in their picture book. Again it is helpful if young authors can work together with a partner, small group, a teacher, a family member or a volunteer to edit their picture books further and make final changes before publishing.

Illustrating and Publishing

Once students have developed their story and are satisfied with the quality of their writing, they are ready to work on a final draft. Before publishing their work, learners need to design the pages of their picture book. There are many ways that students can set up their pages. For example, the content of the story can be divided into sections. Each section can than be organized on a different page with an accompanying illustration. Have students examine page layouts in picture books that are part of the text set collection for ideas. After deciding on the page set-up, students can present the layout for their picture book in the form of a storyboard or diagram, such as the one provided on the next page.

Next, learners can write their final drafts or publish their stories on the computer using a word processing program (e.g., Claris Works®, The Writing Centre® etc.). Students may wish to print or type each page separately, leaving room for illustrations, or publish the entire story as running text, dividing different sections manually (by cutting and pasting) and arranging on separate pages. Students should remember to leave room for margins, borders and illustrations when producing the final draft of their story.

After preparing the text, students are ready to produce the illustrations for their picture book. Encourage the children to use different art materials (e.g., water colors, pastels, pencil crayons, markers etc.) and techniques (e.g., painting, drawing, border patterns etc.) to create their illustrations. Challenge students to include clip art, pop-ups, digital photographs and other forms of technology for the illustrations too. Provide lessons in visual arts on the elements of design (e.g., line, color, space, texture etc.), perspective and other concepts that can assist students with this process.

At the final stage of publication, students should design a cover, order and number the pages, and bind their picture book. A variety of materials and techniques, such as scrapbooks, photo albums, cardboard, fabric, yarn and other paper products, can be used to bind the books together so they can be shared with others.

LEARNING CELEBRATION

Publisher's Fair and Literary Awards Presentation

Once the picture books are published, the students may be interested in sharing their work with others. As a class, organize a book-sharing celebration such as a publisher's fair or a young authors' presentation in the classroom, resource centre or another location (e.g., community centre). Have the children write and deliver invitations to parents,

Picture Book Storyboard

Illustration

Text:_____

_____

Page___

Illustration

Text:_____

_____

Page___

Illustration

Text:_____

_____

Page___

Illustration

Text:_____

_____

Page___

Charlene, Age 11

Premal, Age 11

administrators, volunteers, younger students and teachers in the school. Flyers can also be posted throughout the community. Have the students make decorations and set up displays for the event, including such items as text set collections, picture books published by students, artwork etc.

Prior to the celebration, hold a literary awards contest (similar to the Caldecott and Newberry Awards). As a class, select various categories and criteria that will be used to judge the picture books (e.g., most effective story beginning, most memorable character etc.). Appoint a panel of judges or committee members to read the picture books and select winners in each of the categories. Invite other teachers, parents, guests, administrators and students to make final decisions before the awards presentation.

At the literary celebration, present each student with an award or certificate in a different category. By honoring all students during the literary awards contest, children will begin to to see themselves as young authors and illustrators whose work is worthy of acknowledgement. Celebrating their accomplishments as writers instills them with a sense of pride and motivates them to continue to write, publish work and develop their talent further. During the literary celebration, young authors can read their picture books to guests individually or in small groups as visitors rotate and listen to a variety of stories written by different students.

Consider concluding the literary event with an activity that draws participants together and builds a sense of community. During the literary celebration that I held with my class, participants were able to build on the theme of Interdependence by recording messages on colored strips of paper that explained the importance of people working together and getting along to create a peaceful world. These strips were later attached together to form a paper chain. At the end of the celebration, participants shared their messages with others as they formed a human chain.

EXTENSION ACTIVITIES

Following a picture book celebration, text set collections and children's publications can be used in a variety of other learning experiences. Students can:

- Write book reviews on their classmates' work and publish them in a special magazine edition or newspaper insert about children's literature. These comments can later be included on individual book jackets/covers.
- Share their picture books with community members in seniors' homes, hospitals, local libraries, community centres and bookstores.
- Dramatize scenes from picture books created by peers.
- Design poster advertisements for their publications and plan bookstore or library displays for their text set collections.
- Create a sequel for a picture book in the text set or student collection.

- Invite children's authors and illustrators to the school to share stories and view the picture books.
- Write a letter to the author of a favorite picture book they read in the theme book collection.
- Conduct an author or illustrator study by examining picture books created by the same author or illustrator (e.g., Allan Say, Chris Van Allsburg etc.).
- Display their picture books in the school resource centre or public library for other children to sign out and read.

Picture book units can be developed around a variety of themes related to many subject areas and student interests. Some of these might include:

- Picture books about nature that have an environmental focus;
- Tales about native peoples or ancient civilizations;
- Immigrant stories;
- Books about historical issues (e.g., slavery) and cultural groups (e.g., Black History) — this topic should be handled with great sensitivity;
- Multicultural stories about customs, celebrations and traditions;
- Tales from various countries (e.g., Japan);
- Stories about relationships (e.g., family, friendships);
- Animal tales;
- Books with archetypes and similar characters (e.g., Cinderella stories).

Picture books today provide a rich source of quality literature that appeals to children of all ages. With their meaningful content, impressive use of language and artistic illustrations, they have the power to reach adults too.

Publishing picture books with children is a rewarding experience that carries many benefits. As readers, they acquire a solid understanding of story elements and the writing techniques that authors use to develop them. As writers, they begin to develop vocabulary, creativity, language skills and a writing style all their own. When students see themselves as young authors and illustrators who can produce complex works of fiction, their confidence, pride and literacy skills are enhanced.

By using picture books to teach the art of writing, students are provided with frameworks and models for their own work. While creating their own picture books, the classroom environment becomes a supportive place where writing takes many forms and children produce work for authentic purposes in meaningful and enjoyable ways. In addition to building knowledge and language skills, a picture book unit also provides students with an opportunity to examine a range of themes and topics that relate to different curriculum areas and aspects of life.

Experiences with picture books can have a lasting influence on young people that extends far beyond the classroom. By providing authentic and powerful experiences with theme books and text set collections, young readers can develop an appreciation for an important genre in children's literature, a fascination with language, an interest in illustrations and a joy for reading and writing that can last a lifetime.

CHAPTER THREE

Studying Traditional Folklore

Mythical and legendary short stories that feature characterization and heroes

The world of myths and legends is a fascinating one filled with captivating storylines, an intriguing cast of characters, spectacular settings and epic adventures that entertain readers of all ages. Myths and legends are part of a heritage of traditional folklore that includes stories based on exemplary characters that children are interested in and admire. This makes a theme like Heroes a natural one for exploring these genres. Through a study of myths and legends, young people have an opportunity to become familiar with some traditional story forms, extend their knowledge of story elements — particularly characterization — and explore another form of narrative writing — the short story.

INTRODUCING THE GENRE/THEME

Traditional folklore embraces a rich collection of literature from all over the world that has been passed down over time. Over the years, the customs, beliefs and traditions of cultural groups have been portrayed in songs, stories, myths, legends and other forms of folklore that have been retold in countless ways.

Throughout history, traditional stories, like myths and legends, have served different functions in society. Some provided explanations for natural phenomena like the creation of the world, the changing of the seasons, the rising and setting of the sun and other natural or scientific events that could not otherwise be explained. Other tales were created to justify customs and institutions in society, recount historical events, describe the adventures of an epic character, or teach moral lessons and respectable values. These stories contained elements of fact or fiction. As they were passed down through generations, they had a powerful impact on listeners and readers of all ages. Today, myths, legends and other folkloric stories have become an important part of our literary tradition and cultural heritage. Given their roots in oral culture, these tales are usually not lengthy ones and often appear in the form of a short story.

The characters in myths and legends often embody the superior qualities, values, ideals and morals in society, thereby earning them the respect and admiration of people both past and present. Mythical and legendary characters are often considered to be heroes by virtue of these particular qualities. Examining heroes in traditional folklore can have an important effect on young people. Learning about noble characters from the past will acquaint children with exemplary role models on which to base their own lives. By studying myths and legends, students will become aware of the positive traits and admirable qualities respectable people should possess. Young people will learn to recognize that the actions and accomplishments of these characters reflect ideal human behavior and respected values in society. Apart from Heroes, other important themes can be explored while studying traditional folklore as well.

KNOWLEDGE/SKILL COMPONENTS

Studying traditional folklore from around the world provides students with an opportunity to build knowledge and language skills in a way that extends their experience with literature. By exploring and creating myths and legends through a variety of learning activities, such as those presented in this chapter, students will be able to:

- Examine works of traditional folklore;
- Understand the characteristics of short stories;
- Identify the special features of myths and legends;
- Build knowledge of narrative structure by studying the formats of myths and legends;
- Read, analyze and discuss story elements in myths and legends from around the world;
- Focus on characterization in traditional folklore and recognize specific qualities that portray characters in myths and legends;
- Create their own mythical and legendary characters by incorporating specific features that define them in traditional folklore;
- Develop writing skills by modeling the narrative styles of traditional folklore;
- Employ a variety of pre-writing techniques (e.g., character webbing, plot outlining etc.) to develop different story elements (e.g., setting, plot) for their own myths and legends;
- Write myths and legends in the format of a short story, incorporating the characteristics of each genre into their traditional tale;
- Follow the steps in the writing process to produce their stories;
- Use various drama strategies (e.g., role-playing, improvisation) to present their work to others.

The learning activities in this chapter are designed to introduce students to myths and legends and help them discover the particular characteristics of these forms of traditional folklore. Learners will be able to extend their understanding of narrative structure by examining the way story elements are constructed in myths and legends. In particular, the core activities explore how character development can be central to an intriguing tale. After focusing on traditional folklore related to a particular theme, such as Heroes, students will be able to apply their knowledge of story elements and writing techniques to writing a myth and legend in the form of a short story. Learners will later plan a learning celebration where they can share their traditional stories at a Folklore Convention and Television Talk Show.

Discovering Traditional Folklore

Traditional folklore can take many forms. From a young age, children are delighted by fairy tales, fables, myths, folk tales, legends, tall tales and other traditional stories that have been passed down through generations. Every culture has its own folk stories that can be heard in different languages around the world.

As a class, produce a list of traditional literature forms (e.g., fables, fairy tales, myths, legends etc.). Invite students to share examples of stories from their own family's oral traditions or personal favorites they have encountered over the years. Visit the school or local library and have students collect traditional folklore to feature in a classroom collection. In particular, encourage students to locate myths and legends from all over the world that can be used as models for writing. Provide learners with the opportunity to read stories from the traditional folklore collection.

Examining Short Stories

Throughout history, folk stories have been part of the long-standing oral tradition in many cultures. Out of the growing number of retellings, these traditional tales began to emerge in print. Today, many forms of traditional folklore, such as myths and legends, appear in literature collections and published anthologies, often in the form of a short story.

As a class, revisit the traditional stories in the classroom folklore collection. Locate examples of tales written in the form of a short story. Read several of these short stories to the class. Discuss the characteristics of this genre and produce a list of features of short stories as shown here.

Once students are aware of the characteristics of short stories, begin exploring myths and legends, the traditional folklore formats that will be focused on in this chapter.

Introducing Myths

The world of mythology is a fascinating one for readers to discover. Introduce students to this form of traditional literature by sharing several myths with the class from the folklore collection and invite students to read myths from different cultures on their own. Discuss the characters, setting, plot and other literary elements in the myths. Compare and contrast myths to other forms of literature students may have read.

Features of Short Stories

- Are short in length (only one to several pages long)
- Can easily be read in one sitting
- Contain all of the elements of story (e.g., setting, plot etc.)
- Focus on few characters (protagonist and a few supporting characters)
- Have a short, suspenseful plot that usually builds to the climax quickly
- Feature few, if any, illustrations
- Include different genres (e.g., folklore, mystery, science-fiction etc.)
- May be compiled into a published anthology or collection

After encountering several myths in the collection, learners may become aware of their specific features. In cooperative groups, ask students to brainstorm the characteristics of a myth. As a class, make a list of these qualities, as illustrated on this page, and post them for student reference.

Introducing Legends

Legends are traditional tales that describe the adventures and famous deeds of important characters whose life stories have been exaggerated. Introduce the genre by sharing a collection of legends from around the world with the class and inviting students to read these adventure tales on their own.

After encountering the fascinating characters and realistic settings that these stories provide, young people may be able to identify the characteristics of this genre. Have students discuss the specific characteristics of a legend with others. Later, produce a list of these qualities as a class and record them as shown on this page.

CORE ACTIVITIES

Studying myths and legends, especially through a theme such as heroes, provides a great opportunity to explore characterization in detail. The creation of strong main characters and interesting supporting characters is often central to the development of the setting and plot for these and many other types of stories. This connection between characterization and the development of other story elements is examined in more detail in the activities that follow.

Focusing on Myths

Exploring Mythical Characters

The world of mythology is filled with fascinating characters whose lives and epic adventures capture readers young and old alike. The pages of myths are filled with the exploits of gods, goddesses, heroes, heroines, monsters, mortals and other symbolic figures. These characters frequently have an important area of responsibility and are represented by various distinctive symbols.

In order for students to discover these mythical characters, provide them with picture books, anthologies, reference books and other resource materials based on mythology. In cooperative groups, have students research the prominent characters in world myths and fill in a recording sheet like the one featured on the opposite page.

Once the groups have completed their charts, review the list of important characters in world myths. Afterwards, ask the students to select one of the gods or goddesses they have researched and design a

Characters in Mythology

Name of Character	Type of Myth	Area of Responsibility	Symbol(s)
Hades	Greek	The Underworld	Helmet Metal Jewels
Jupiter	Roman	Ruler of the earth and sky	Thunderbolt

Grade Six Students

Zeshan, Age 11

business card for this mythical character outlining his/her responsibilities and featuring the symbols associated with this literary figure.

Finally, have the students compare and contrast the characters in one type of myth (e.g., Greek) with their counterparts in another (e.g., Roman, Celtic etc.). Encourage students to identify gods, goddesses and other mythical figures from early civilizations (e.g., Aztec) and cultural or religious traditions (e.g., Hinduism). As a class, discuss the qualities that set mythological figures apart from characters in other narratives (e.g., novels, picture books etc.) that students may have read. For example, mythical characters may:

- Be based on real people from long ago or be imaginary;
- Possess supernatural powers or special skills;
- Have unusual physical characteristics (e.g., half human, half animal);
- Live forever (i.e., be immortal).

Creating a Mythical Character

Like other forms of narrative, a myth is based on the life of a lead character. After discovering the main characters in world myths, students can create their own mythical character. In order to develop this important figure, provide learners with the following activity:

- Explain that new gods or goddesses are invited to appear before the World Council, a powerful group of mythical figures, and that members of this prestigious body must decide whether or not a new deity should be admitted into its important group.
- Ask students to create a new god or goddess and assign this figure with an important duty needed to run society in either the ancient or modern world.
- Have the students write a detailed description of this new deity and explain his/her role or responsibility. Also, have the students describe the symbols associated with this mythical character, along with other aspects of his/her life.
- Challenge the students to imagine that they are the deity and must appear before the panel of mythical figures who sit on the World Council. Tell them that they will need to introduce themselves and explain in detail why they should be admitted into this powerful group.

To help students with this activity, suggest that they make a list of features or personal information for the deity, including name, family history, powers, symbols, famous deeds etc. Encourage students to use the planning sheet provided on the opposite page or another writing strategy (e.g., character web) to develop their character. Invite students to share their character profiles with others and later, display their work in an interesting way. The students in my class created a puzzle featuring a different mythical character on each puzzle piece.

After students have produced their mythical characters, have them work in partners to improvise chance encounters (including a formal introduction and discussion) among these prominent figures.

David, Age 11

Creating a Mythical Character

Name of the Mythical Character: _____

Physical Appearance: _____

_____

_____

Personal History or Family Background: _____

_____

_____

Area of Responsibility: _____

_____

Strengths and Weaknesses: _____

_____

_____

Special Powers: _____

_____

Symbols: _____

_____

Dwelling Place: _____

_____

Reason for Being Famous: _____

_____

_____

Other Interesting Facts: _____

_____

_____

_____

_____

Finally, invite each student to present his/her mythical character to the class while in role. Select a panel of judges (e.g., parents, support staff, administrators, community volunteers, librarian, other students etc.) to determine which mythical character will join the prestigious group of gods and goddesses on the World Council. Conduct a debate about which deity to admit as a new member. Once the judges have made their decision, have a representative announce the selection to the class. Afterwards, conduct an inauguration ceremony in honor of this new member.

Developing Other Characters for a Myth

Apart from the protagonist, the pages of a myth are filled with other dramatic characters like gods, goddesses, heroes, mortals, animals and supernatural creatures who also play vital roles in the story. Once students have developed a lead character, they should select other prominent figures who will appear in their myth. To assist with character development, ask learners to reflect on the following questions:

- Who are the other characters in your myth?
- Are your characters gods, goddesses, heroes, monsters, mortals, animals or supernatural beings?
- What do these figures look like?
- What do they wear?
- Do they walk, talk or eat?
- Are they strange? In what ways?
- Do they have superhuman qualities or special powers? What are they?
- What are their personalities like?
- What relationships do they have to the main character in the myth?

As students focus on the element of characterization, encourage them to use a variety of writing techniques and narrative strategies to develop this story element and record their ideas (e.g., webs, lists, charts, character sketches/profiles). The students in my class used file cards to record information about each supporting character in their myth. Their stories were filled with an intriguing cast of characters, such as fearless monsters, immortal gods and other mysterious creatures who challenged or aided the mythical lead character.

Creating a Setting for a Myth

As readers explore the world of mythology they often encounter fascinating places and unique locations that mark the setting of these traditional stories. Have students revisit the myths they have read and produce a list of interesting settings where these folkloric tales have taken place. These may include:

- Another world (e.g., underworld, planet, sky);
- Locations around the globe (e.g., different countries);
- Sites in ancient civilizations (e.g., town, city, state etc.);
- Universal settings (e.g., ocean).

In order to decide on the location for their myth, invite students to close their eyes and use their imagination to create the story setting. Guide them through the visualization process by asking leading questions such as:

- Imagine your myth is going to take place in a new world. Will it be an underworld, a new planet or a secret place on earth?
- How will your world look, feel, sound and smell?
- Will it be light or dark, hot or cold?
- Will this be a world of sound or a silent place?
- Where will this place be located? In another town, city, country or place in the ancient world?
- What are the distinct features of this place? Are there interesting landmarks or natural formations that are part of the scenery?
- Why do your characters belong in this place?

Following the guided imagery experience, ask students to describe their world in detail to others. Encourage listeners to close their eyes and envision the place being described. Later, have students recreate their main story setting in a visual arts experience. Provide the class with a variety of materials and art forms (e.g., pastels, watercolors, murals etc.) from which to choose. Finally, ask students to produce a map of the story setting and write a detailed description for their myth.

Planning the Action for a Myth

Like other traditional stories, myths are often based on action and adventure. The event-filled pages shape the story plot and involve characters in a variety of activities. In order to develop the action for their myth, have students revisit the collection of world myths they have read and examine reference books describing life in early civilizations. As a class, produce a list of purposes for the myths they have read. These might include:

- A creation story;
- An explanation of a natural event or scientific phenomenon (e.g., change of seasons, the sun's rising, the evolution of fire or light);
- An adventure tale of a hero;
- A story of the relationship between gods and mortals;
- A story describing human behavior or a cultural practice.

Ask students to select a focus for their myth from the list generated.

In order to plan the action for their stories, challenge learners to produce a list of activities that mythological characters or people in ancient societies were involved in (e.g., farming, weaving, building etc.). By examining the personal enterprises, businesses and industries that have existed in world cultures throughout history, students will be able to establish the activities that will take place in their own myth. To assist with plot development, ask students the following questions:

- What happens in your world?
- What events will take place in your myth?
- What unusual and usual activities will occur?

- Is there farming in your world?
- Are there businesses or factories?
- What do the children do?
- What do the adults do in this society?

After reading a variety of world myths, students may be aware of the complex storylines and conflicts that emerge in these traditional stories. Challenge them to think about the intricate problems or compound issues that may develop in their own myth. To help them generate ideas, ask students to think about the following questions:

- What will be the major conflict in your myth?
- What role will the characters play in this conflict?
- What other problems may arise?
- Which characters will oppose each other?
- How do you plan to resolve this conflict?

After considering all of the elements that will affect the plot of their story (e.g., activities, conflicts), have students produce an outline of the events that will take place in their myth.

Writing a Myth

After focusing on the different story elements that are part of traditional narratives, students can incorporate the ideas they developed into their own short myth. As a class, review the characteristics of both a myth and a short story. Learners should incorporate the ideas developed previously into their short stories by revisiting the lessons that focused on developing different elements of the myth (e.g., mythical characters, other characters, setting, plot etc.).

Encourage students to refer to the writing strategies used earlier to develop the different story elements (e.g., character webs, index cards, maps, plot summaries, outlines etc.) when planning their story and producing a rough copy. Remind students to construct their myth in the format of a short story by following the steps in the writing process (see Chapter 2). Where needed, provide mini-lessons to help students generate story ideas and develop technical writing skills (e.g., paragraphs, sentence structure etc.). After producing a rough copy of their myth, have students work with others to revise and edit their narratives. Once final changes are made, learners can publish their short stories (using the computer, handwriting, printing or another technique).

My own students produced myths in the form of short stories related to the theme of Heroes. Some of them wrote creation stories, adventure tales or story sequels to myths they had read. In their sequels to *The Twelve Labors of Hercules*, for example, young writers recounted fascinating tales of Hercules obtaining a precious crystal guarded by the six-headed dog named Charibus or rescuing Persephone from the dreaded Underworld and its dark ruler, Hades. As part of his thirteenth labour, one writer even challenged Hercules to read one hundred books on different cultures, religions, stories and historical events, despite the fact the hero was illiterate.

The 13th labour of Heracles was to read one hundred books on different cultures, religions, stories and historical events. There was one problem, however Heracles did not know how to read. He went to school and tried to learn how to read and it did not help him. He tried and tried but it could not help him. He went to at least three schools a day. One in the morning, one in the afternoon, and one in the evening. This still didn't help him.

In his first spelling test Heracles scored 0 - out of 5. Everyone knew that he wasn't very bright. The King thought that it was a bit hard so he said "I want you to tell me 20 bedtime stories. That was a lot for Heracles. He attended classes, but nothing would help. One day Heracles was asked to read to his class. Heracles started to sweat. He really wanted to attack the teacher but then all his labours would go down the drain. As the teacher and the class were waiting, his teacher knew that he could not read so she wrote one word down on the blackboard the word was "I" Heracles said "E". Everyone laughed and laughed. He had never been that embarrassed in his whole life. He kept on trying and trying he just couldn't read. Everyone thought that he wanted to show off his muscles and prove that he is so strong, because he did not tell anyone about the 13th labour he kept on trying and trying. The king said, "we will just forget about the 13th labour and we will not put it in our history!

Harpreet, Age 11

Focusing on Legends

Exploring Legendary Characters

Legends are filled with epic characters whose lives are marked by adventure and intrigue. Have students research legendary characters using picture books, short story anthologies, reference books, films, Internet sites and other resource materials. As a class, produce a list of legendary characters from all around the world (e.g., Europe, China, Middle East, Japan, India, Africa etc.), similar to the one shown here.

Legendary Characters

- King Arthur
- Merlin
- Sir Lancelot
- Robin Hood
- Joan of Arc
- Guinevere
- Saint George
- Sir Gawain
- Mulan
- Aladdin
- Ali Baba
- Sundiata
- Knights of the Round Table
- Ishikawa
- Laura Secord
- Cleopatra
- Vasilisa

Invite students to read a variety of legends from long ago (see bibliography for a detailed book list) and examine the lives of the legendary characters in these classic stories. Ask learners to complete an information chart, like the one featured on the following page, while working in cooperative groups.

Afterwards, have students work in pairs to assume the role of their favorite legendary character or a news reporter and conduct an interview for a local newspaper or television station.

As a class, compare and contrast the lives of legendary characters from around the world, noting similarities and differences in their childhood, training, special qualities and famous deeds. Challenge students to identify important features that symbolize all legendary characters. In my class, the students discovered that many legends are based on the life of a heroic character. After discussing the characteristics of a hero, the class produced a list of special features, like the one shown below.

The Portrait of a Hero

A hero:

- Can be either male or female.
- Has special qualities such as courage, strength, kindness and intelligence.
- Must solve a problem, overcome an obstacle or achieve a goal.
- Performs heroic deeds to save others.
- Earns the respect and admiration of people for his/her actions and qualities.
- May become famous for performing a specific deed (e.g., defeating an evil character).

Legendary Characters from around the World

Name of Character	Childhood & Training	Personal Qualities/ Characteristics	Famous Deeds

Creating a Legendary Character

After examining the element of characterization in legends, students may be eager to create a legendary character of their own. As a class, begin by discussing the central importance of legendary characters in traditional folklore and produce a list of common characteristics that define these noble figures. These may include:

- Important childhood experiences or behaviors that had a direct impact on their future life;
- Formal education or informal training that prepared them for their adult role in society;
- Special qualities and characteristics that earned them respect and admiration from others;
- Important people (assistants, mentors etc.) who had a strong influence on their life;
- Courageous deed(s) that made them famous.

Remind students that their characters should be non-violent and work on the side of good to defeat evil. Encourage young writers to use the planning sheet shown on the following page to record their ideas before producing a character sketch and summary. Indicate that all aspects of their profile, including the person's actions, personality traits and dialogue (speech) should reflect a consistently positive portrayal of the legendary character they have created.

In my class, the students produced detailed character profiles of legendary heroes from the Middle Ages using various narrative techniques and writing strategies.

Developing Other Characters for a Legend

The pages of a legend are filled with other assorted characters who contribute to the action, suspense and adventure of the story. Ask students to recount the lives of legendary characters in traditional tales they have read and identify other people who played an important part in these noble figures' lives and the stories themselves. These might include:

- Family members, relatives and friends;
- Mentors, helpers and assistants;
- Enemies, rivals and opponents.

Have students generate a list of other characters for their legend by developing a character web similar to the one shown here.

Arlando, Age 9

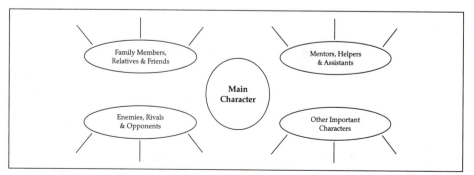

Creating a Legendary Character

Create your own legendary character who may have lived long ago. Describe different aspects of the character's life. Use the planning guide below to develop your character.

Name of Character: _____

Social Class/Background: _____

Childhood: _____

_____

_____

Education/Training: _____

_____

_____

_____

Personal Characteristics: _____

_____

_____

Special Qualities: _____

_____

_____

Assistants/Helpers: _____

_____

Famous Deeds: _____

Write a character profile (descriptive paragraph) of this legendary figure.

_____

_____

_____

_____

_____

Produce a sketch or portrait illustrating the legendary character described above.

In order to help students develop the individual qualities and characteristics of each supporting character, encourage them to include specific details (e.g., appearance, personal traits, special powers, important deeds etc.) on the character web too.

Creating a Setting for a Legend

The legendary world is filled with imaginary places, realistic locations and universal settings in countries around the globe. Have students revisit legends they have read, discuss the various settings of these traditional stories and identify the historical time periods they are based on (e.g., Medieval Times, Empirical Era, Colonial Period etc.). Encourage learners to close their eyes and envision many of the settings described in traditional legends.

Ask students to create a setting or settings for their own legendary story by selecting the country, places and time period for the traditional tale they will write. Challenge learners to conduct library research to discover information on the historical era or country where their legend will take place, and to later include this factual content in their short story. Encourage students to represent the various settings of their legend in charcoal drawings, watercolor paintings or other visual arts forms. Later, ask learners to write a detailed description of their legendary setting or settings.

Planning the Action for a Legend

The events of a legend are often filled with action, suspense and excitement. Before developing the plot for their story, have students consider the following important details in the legends they have read:

Plot Outline		
Goal(s)	Problems/ Conflicts	Main Events (listed in order)
Obstacles	Solutions and Outcomes	Lessons and Morals to be Learned

- Goal of the legendary character;
- Problems/conflicts to be overcome;
- Main events in the legend;
- Obstacles encountered along the way;
- Final outcomes and solutions;
- Lessons and morals to be learned.

Invite the children to share examples from legendary tales from around the world by retelling memorable events and exciting plot developments. Ask young writers to plan the action and order of events in their own legend by filling in a plot outline like the one shown in the diagram.

Writing a Legend

Legends are fascinating stories that both entertain readers and reveal important lessons about life and humanity. They often use exaggeration to make the story more interesting by embellishing details and fabricating events. After reading a variety of traditional legends and developing story elements like character, setting and plot, students should be ready to write their own legend using the short story format they encountered earlier.

One day when Sir Dragon Heart was a child he asked his parents if he could be a page. He wanted to be a page, but his parents didn't want him to learn to be a knight. So one night he left his home and went to live in a neighbouring castle with a knight.

Within months, he had become a page and then a squire. Since Sir Dragon Heart was the best squire ever, he went to train with one of the knights of the round table. After his training was complete, Sir Dragon Heart became a knight of the round table. His helpers were Sir Adrian, Sir Amaran, and Sir Arlando who were also knights of the round table.

In one of his first battles, Sir Dragon Heart went to the forest to fight the black knight. During the fight, Sir Dragon Heart's sword broke. Then he went to see the Lady of the Lake. He asked the Lady of the Lake if she could give him a sword. She gave him two swords that were identical.

The Lady explained, "You will need two swords to fight the Black Knight. One will be a fake sword. The other will be the real one. Remember the one in the right hand is real."

When the black knight found out the power of the sword that Sir Dragon Heart had received from the Lady of the Lake, he sent an army out to get the sword. When they found Sir Dragon Heart they took the fake sword believing it was the real one. Then the black knight's sword lost its power and became a regular sword.

Later, the black knight saw King Arthur and attacked him. Sir Dragon Heart and his helpers went to help King Arthur. The black knight was about to kill King Arthur, but Sir Dragon Heart saved him and defeated the black knight with the sword he got from The Lady of the Lake. When King Arthur died Sir Dragon Heart became the king.

Ajit, Age 9

Sheriza, Age 11

First, have learners review the characteristics of both the short stories and the legends they have read. Discuss the unique aspects of these genres including the format, the characters and their admirable traits or special qualities, the story setting (e.g., place, time period), significant events (e.g., famous deeds), problems or conflicts, solutions to conflicts, and the values and lessons revealed in the traditional tales they have studied. Young writers should then select a topic for their legend related to the chosen theme, such as Heroes.

Have students follow the steps in the writing process to plan their legendary story. Learners should incorporate the ideas presented previously into their short stories by revisiting the lessons that focused on developing different elements of a legend (e.g., legendary characters, other characters, setting, plot etc.). Afterwards, have students produce a rough copy, revise/edit their short story and publish their final work. Students may wish to create a special thematic cover and/or include appropriate illustrations.

Over the years, my students have produced fascinating legends based on imaginary characters, heroes and events from the Middle Ages. Some young writers crafted their short stories into works of historical fiction that revealed aspects of Medieval life within their legendary tales. Others even challenged traditional stereotypes in their epic stories:

> *Long ago there was a princess who was unusual from the day she was born. Princess Laura never did anything she was told. She always did the opposite. Princess Laura never bothered to learn to sew and make medicine. Instead she enjoyed riding horses, climbing trees, and most of all learning to fight. Her older brother who was a knight named Pete taught her to fight…*

> *Mary, Age 11*

LEARNING CELEBRATION

Folklore Convention and Television Talk Show

Children and adults of all ages enjoy listening to and reading traditional stories like myths and legends. In order to celebrate the efforts and accomplishments of young writers who developed traditional stories of their own, plan a "folklore convention" with the class where students can share their myths and legends with others.

Prior to the convention, brainstorm a list of awards that can be presented to the participants and prepare a series of trophies, certificates, medals or other prizes that can be used to honor the guests. Invite participants to attend the special event dressed as a legendary or mythical character.

During the convention, encourage members to introduce themselves in role and improvise the conversations that might take place between folkloric characters from different historical time periods, cultural backgrounds, societies and traditional literature forms. Encourage guests to read the myths and legends that students have written. Later, conduct an awards ceremony where all legendary or mythical characters are honored for a special quality they possess or a noble deed they performed in society.

Following the folklore convention, conduct a television talk show and invite participants to be part of a panel discussion highlighting the features of traditional folklore — particularly detailed characterization. Encourage guests (e.g., administrators, parents, volunteers, other students etc.) to act as hosts, while the students themselves portray the characters they created or researched in myths and legends they had read. Invite other visitors to serve as audience members and pose their own questions to the panel of distinguished guests. At the end of the celebration, have young authors discuss their writing experiences with others and invite guests to share their opinions of the myths and legends the students created.

EXTENSION ACTIVITIES

Studying traditional folklore can lead to a variety of learning experiences that integrate many skills and disciplines. Students can engage in different activities based on the myths, legends and other tales they have read and the traditional tales they have published. Throughout or after the unit, the students can:

- Create alternative endings, story sequels or other myths and legends based on traditional stories they have read.
- Write a modern epic adventure featuring mythical or legendary characters from traditional folklore.
- Imagine they are a storyteller living in the past and retell the epic events in the life of one of the mythical or legendary characters found in the traditional tales they have studied.
- Recount the epic adventures in a mythical or legendary character's life in a series of diary entries or a scrapbook.
- Watch movie clips from modern films about mythical and legendary characters from different historical periods and cultural backgrounds. Compare and contrast the way story elements are depicted in the film(s) to the way they are portrayed in traditional folklore that has been published.
- Select two or more myths or legends from different cultures. Compare and contrast the narrative elements in these traditional tales.
- Dramatize a myth or legend from the traditional folklore collection or a tale written by the students themselves.
- Design advertisements, posters, dioramas and other works of art (e.g., mural) to advertise or illustrate their traditional story.
- Compare and contrast the lives of two or more mythical or legendary characters from different cultural backgrounds and historical time periods.
- Read different versions of the same myth or legend and make comparisons.

- Write letters to their favorite mythical or legendary characters.
- Produce a script, play or television sitcom based on a traditional story they have read or written.
- Share the traditional stories they have written with members of the community by visiting libraries, bookstores, hospitals and seniors' homes where young writers can read their tales to others.
- Study the historical time periods and world cultures where traditional tales like myths and legends originated (e.g., Medieval Times, Ancient Greece etc.).
- Explore other themes in traditional literature collections (e.g., role of women).
- Read and write other forms of traditional folklore (e.g., fairy tales, fables, folk tales, tall tales etc.).

The world of traditional folklore offers young people a cultural experience that enriches their lives and extends their understanding of story. Studying traditional literature, such as myths and legends, provides students with the opportunity to work with different genres, build knowledge of narrative elements and develop language skills in a sophisticated way. As young writers produce mythical and legendary short stories based on a particular theme, such as Heroes, their understanding of narrative structure, story elements and literature forms grows. Modeling the narrative styles of traditional folklore helps students develop their writing techniques, apply the characteristics of specific genres to their work and understand aspects of traditional literature that influence the story world.

Over time, universal stories like myths and legends have become an important part of our cultural heritage. These traditional tales contain an array of characters, themes, archetypes and motifs on which other works of fiction are based. By examining these folkloric stories, students can learn to understand allusions to classical literature and recognize references to familiar characters and plots in other stories and novels they read as well as television programs and movies they watch. By constructing myths and legends filled with captivating characters, dynamic settings, fascinating plots and compelling themes, young writers are able to add to the growing collection of folkloric tales available today.

CHAPTER FOUR

Creating Poetry

The production of a classroom anthology that highlights
literary forms and the environment

Visit a playground and you will be delighted by the sounds of poetry
you hear all around you. Children are natural poets who enjoy playing
with words and using language in a spirited way. Young people can
experience the pleasure of poetry in classrooms too. Incorporating
poetry into the curriculum can lead to meaningful learning experiences
for children of all ages.

Encounters with poetry allow students to build language skills and
knowledge in a sophisticated way. Listening to, reading and creating
poems on a range of topics and experiences can strengthen children's
imaginative capacities and help them connect facts and the aesthetic
dimension. Students can acquire experience with meaning, develop
higher-level thinking and deepen their understanding of the world
through poetry.

Nature can inspire some of the most profound works of poetry.
Children's fascination with nature makes the theme of the Environment
an ideal choice for creating a poetry collection.

INTRODUCING THE GENRE/THEME

Poetry is filled with enchantment, beauty and enjoyment that entertains
readers of all ages. Young people are exposed to the magical sounds of
poetry through nursery and schoolyard rhymes, chants, songs and
games. Children from all cultures enjoy the rhythm of language and the
melodic verses of poetry.

Although most students have encountered poetry naturally
throughout their lives, many of them do not write poetry easily.
Through meaningful classroom experiences with poetry, students can
learn to express themselves using this art form. Children should have
opportunities to read, listen to, respond to and write poems about topics
they find compelling. Young people are captivated by the world around
them. Developing a poetry study based on a theme, such as the
Environment, allows students to explore aspects of the natural world,
develop an appreciation for the environment, and discover the wonder
and potential of poetry. Many other topics and themes can also be used
successfully to engage students in a poetry study.

Experiences with poetry enable children to develop knowledge and skills in all areas of language (listening, speaking, reading and writing), as well as in the arts. By participating in a variety of poetry activities, such as those offered in this chapter, students will be able to:

- Develop an understanding of print, language forms, word patterns and the functions of writing;
- Understand concepts presented in works of poetry;
- Acquire a knowledge of poetry conventions;
- Develop new insights and ways of understanding the world;
- Improve listening skills by delighting in works of poetry;
- Enhance oral language and presentation skills (e.g., through choral reading of poems);
- Strengthen reading skills (e.g., making inferences, judgements);
- Make connections between letters and sounds (especially in pattern poetry);
- Interpret texts and make meaning from print;
- Extend their imagination and expand their vocabulary;
- Develop higher-level thinking skills (e.g., analysis, synthesis etc.);
- Produce subjective, personal responses to works of poetry;
- Deepen their emotions and enhance their experiences through poetry activities;
- Create works of poetry using a variety of forms;
- Use language creatively to convey meaning, messages, ideas and concepts in a poetic way;
- Explore language functions and uses through word-play;
- Use patterning, ordering and sequencing to organize thoughts into poems;
- Manipulate words, sounds and meanings to fit patterns;
- Use descriptive language and imagery in their poetry writing;
- Apply poetic devices to their work (e.g., use parallel structures);
- Use sophisticated literary tools and stylistic devices (e.g., metaphor, simile etc.) to enhance their writing;
- Develop their own style of poetry writing (e.g., free verse);
- Develop an aesthetic appreciation of the world;
- Acquire a love for language, an enjoyment for words and an appreciation for poetry as an art form.

The learning activities in this chapter are designed to introduce students to a different style of writing and an art form. Students will have an opportunity to read poetry related to a chosen theme, such as the Environment, and respond to poetry in a variety of ways. The teaching strategies provided will also guide learners as they discover the characteristics of different types of poetry and apply knowledge of these poetry conventions to their own writing. Students will present their poems in the form of a thematic classroom anthology and plan a learning celebration where poems can be shared at a Poetry Reading.

Creating the Environment

Introduce students to the delights of poetry by immersing them in a world of imaginative literature. In order to create an environment where children can encounter poetry all around them through literature collections, classroom displays and authentic learning experiences, you may wish to try one of these activities.

The Poetry Corner

Establish a setting in the classroom where students can read, respond to and write poems. Have the children create a "Poetry Corner" complete with a rocking chair, pillows, sofa or rug, and a collection of poetry books related to a chosen theme, such as the Environment. Invite students to spend time there, reading items in the collection. Provide art materials and journals that learners can use to express their personal responses to poetry. Include a variety of paper products (e.g., decorative stationary), writing supplies (e.g., colored pens, calligraphy markers etc.) and a computer that students can use to compose their own poems. Encourage the students to bring in objects that may inspire poetry writing and display them at the Poetry Corner. Enrich the learning environment with visual displays of poetry too.

"Poet Tree" Bulletin Board

One way to create an atmosphere in the classroom where poetry can come to life is to design a bulletin board display featuring a tree where students can attach poems about the Environment, or another theme, to the branches. This collection can feature the works of famous poets, selections from children's anthologies or poems produced by the students themselves. Encourage students to contribute phrases and poems at any time. Setting up a "poet tree" as a permanent feature in the classroom can illustrate the pleasure of words and the language of poetry throughout the year.

Discovering Poetry

Poetry provides an open door for sharing stories, expressing emotions, creating images, using powerful language and entertaining readers young and old alike. Invite children to discover the world of poetry by surrounding them with poems and having them interact with poems in a natural and personal way. Here are some activities to get started.

Creating a Poetry Display

Poetry exists all around us. As shown in the box on this page, poetry can take many different forms.

Invite students to share examples of poetry from their daily lives by recounting nursery and schoolyard rhymes, reading greeting cards,

---

Sources of Poetry

- Poetry books
- Poetry anthologies
- Songbooks
- Sheet music
- Hymnbooks
- Song lyrics
- Greeting cards
- Advertisements
- Slogans
- Nursery rhymes
- Traditional ballads
- Poetic verse
- Schoolyard rhymes
- Chants
- Lyrical prose

examining song lyrics and reciting poems dealing with a common topic or theme. Arrange a trip to the school or local library where students can gather their own poetry collections. Ask learners to locate poetry books and anthologies on a range of topics related to a chosen theme, such as the Environment. Encourage students to bring in poems and poetry books from home to feature in the classroom collection. Assemble these literary works in a poetry display. Invite students to sign out books from this collection, read them independently and enjoy them with others.

The Poetry Graffiti Wall

Poetry carries many different meanings for those who read it. Invite children to share their impressions of poetry with the class by distributing file cards or paper strips to the students and asking them to write down what comes to mind when they think about poetry or a poem. Encourage learners to use both literal and figurative language to explain the meaning of poetry (e.g., words arranged in a rhyming pattern; an imaginative way of seeing the world etc.). Students can create symbols and illustrations to accompany the words and phrases they produce.

After brainstorming characteristics of the genre in this way, have students prepare a graffiti wall by posting their definitions of poetry on a bulletin board, wall chart, wipe board or other visual display. Invite learners to share their contributions with others. As a class, arrange the items on the graffiti wall into a poem or poems that explain the meaning of poetry.

Introducing Types of Poetry

Poetry is one of the most expressive and creative forms of writing. By drawing on their imagination and experiences, poets are able to develop ideas, communicate messages and convey emotions using different poetic styles. As students encounter poems in collections, anthologies and other sources, they will also realize that poetry can take many identifiable forms. As a class, produce a list of poetic forms similar to the one shown here. Ask students to locate examples and describe the patterns and functions of different types of poetry. Many of these forms will be examined later in the chapter.

CORE ACTIVITIES

Reading Poetry

Share an enthusiasm and enjoyment for poetry by reading it aloud. Provide opportunities for students to listen to a variety of poems throughout the year. Encounters with poetry in this way will enable children to experience various forms and styles before writing their own. To engage students in read-aloud experiences, you may wish to:

- Introduce young people to different types of poetry such as:
  - narrative;

Types Of Poetry

- Acrostics
- Cinquains
- Couplets
- Limericks
- Lyrics
- Concrete
- Pattern
- Free Verse
- Rhyming
- Humorous
- Image
- Found
- Triads
- Syllable
- Quatrains
- Diamantes
- Haiku
- Tanka
- Five W
- Narrative
- Traditional
- Modern
- Empathy
- Puzzle
- Imitative
- Autobio-
  graphical
- Triolets
- Contrast

- humorous;
- free verse;
- rhyming;
- traditional;
- modern.
- Share poetry with the class as part of a thematic unit of study by locating poems dealing with a particular theme such as the Environment that are written by different poets.
- Use poems to introduce concepts, conclude lessons and enrich learning experiences.
- Provide models for reading poetry aloud by employing different elements, such as timing, tempo, volume, tone and feeling.

Once the students have listened to a lot of poetry read aloud, plan learning activities where children can read poetry both aloud and on their own. To do this:

- Schedule time for independent poetry reading.
- Ask students to keep a list of the poems they have read.
- Encourage children to copy their favorite poems into a response journal or writing notebook.
- Provide opportunities for students to practise reading their poems aloud by sharing them with a partner.
- Challenge learners to use different strategies to convey the meaning of poems when reading aloud. Effective read-aloud techniques may include:
  - finding the emotional tone (general feeling) of the poem;
  - changing the pace throughout the reading;
  - selecting the correct phrasing;
  - pausing at different points (using punctuation as a guide);
  - altering the pitch (tone);
  - emphasizing certain words or parts;
  - expressing words with clarity;
  - regulating the volume;
  - modifying the voice to add variety.
- Invite children to present different poetic works to the class.

Read-aloud experiences engage students in bringing the print to life. Shared reading activities and independent activities can help children develop an enjoyment and appreciation for poetry too.

Responding to Poetry

Poetry is an expressive form of literature that invites response. The sounds, patterns, forms and meanings are meant to be enjoyed by others. Children should engage in a variety of poetry experiences in classrooms and beyond. By engaging in a wide variety of response activities, children will be able to articulate their understanding and response to poetry in different ways. Students can explore possible meanings, learn the forms, structures and functions of poetry and delight in this literary art form. Response activities can also help students consolidate their understanding of different forms and styles before creating their own works of poetry.

Discussions

Students can explore their personal responses to poetry through discussion. After reading a poem or listening to one read aloud, learners can participate in lively discussions surrounding the meaning of the text in small groups or as a class. Students can be invited to share their personal reactions and interpretations with others. Learners can challenge each other's observations by asking questions that lead to deeper analysis. These questions may deal with the poet's word choices, writing style and/or message. Alternatively, students can discuss the images in a poem or relate the experiences evoked by a poem.

Journals

Children can also explore their personal responses to poetry through journal writing in a learning log or response journal. This record may include:

- A list of poetry books students have read;
- Initial impressions of a poem;
- Observations;
- Personal interpretations;
- A collection of favorite poems;
- Impressive words, phrases or lines from poetry selections;
- Questions to be raised in literary discussions;
- Ideas for poetry writing.

Arts Experiences

Sabrina, Age 11

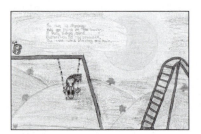

Manisha, Age 11

Encounters with poetry can be extended into arts experiences as well. Students can express their responses to poems through music, visual arts, dance and drama.

In music, for example, children can experiment with poetry selections using sound effects, instruments, clapping and other rhythmic patterns. Young people may also wish to create a musical accompaniment for a poem they have read. In visual arts, learners can recreate images and feelings evoked by poems in drawings, paintings and other works of art. Children can illustrate poems written by their favorite poets too.

The meaning of poems can also be recreated using drama and dance techniques such as mime, tableaux, creative movement and dance sequences. To engage students in drama experiences, you may wish to:

- Assign small groups to present poems as choral readings.
- Provide opportunities for students to discuss the meaning of poems they selected before presenting them.
- Challenge students to recreate the experiences, events, feelings, motives and messages in poems to others using symbols.
- Encourage students to experiment with different strategies to present their poems effectively as a group. Poems can be read:

    – in unison;
    – in two-part arrangements;
    – line-by-line by different readers;
    – in a call and response format;
    – accompanied by movement, sound effects or music.
- Invite students to assume the roles of different characters in a poem and present it as a role-play.

Writing Poetry

Writing poetry enables young people to experience the world through a new dimension and express their thoughts, ideas and emotions in an aesthetic way. Poetry is also a sophisticated tool for teaching different literary or stylistic devices, grammar conventions and elements of writing. Opportunities for creating poetry may emerge at different moments throughout the year. Provide open invitations for children to write poems whenever they find their voice and inspiration.

Before producing their own works of poetry in a variety of forms, students should participate in a number of pre-writing activities. These might include:

- Brainstorming aspects of the chosen theme and presenting ideas in a word web or concept map as shown in the example on this page.
- Generating a list of rhyming words associated with topics related to the chosen theme.
- Engaging in word-play and vocabulary-building exercises (e.g., creating antonyms and synonyms).
- Examining the use of poetic devices and stylistic tools (e.g., similes, metaphors, imagery, personification, contrast, comparison) in poems and other forms of literature.
- Practising the use of stylistic tools (e.g., writing similes, comparisons, personifications) before writing their own poems.
- Exploring the rhythms, refrains, repetitions and verses in a variety of poems, songs, chants and games.
- Reviewing the characteristics, patterns and structures of various forms of poetry by reading several examples.

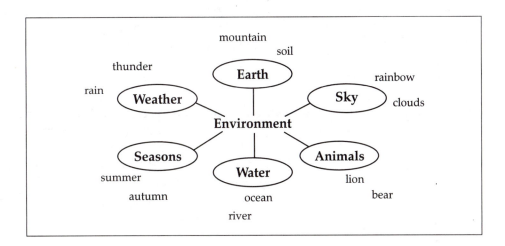

- Gathering ideas for poetry writing from works of literature (e.g., picture books, novels, folktales) that connect to a particular theme or collecting objects that serve as stimuli for poetry writing.

Students can then use the general writing tips provided below to help them consolidate the knowledge and skills necessary for creating their own works of poetry in a variety of forms.

General Poetry Writing Tips

- Write collective poems as a class, in a small group or with a partner when a new form or style is introduced.
- Write from personal experience wherever possible about aspects of the chosen theme.
- Select a topic for your poem that interests you.
- Generate words on your topic for all parts of speech (nouns, verbs, adjectives).
- Select a format or style of poetry and write a rough draft.
- Use patterns, shapes and formats from structured poems as a framework for your ideas.
- Add stylistic tools and literary devices to make your poems come alive.
- Organize your ideas into a poetic frame (e.g., verse).
- Use standard punctuation in your poems or no punctuation at all.
- Read your poem aloud to check the rhyming scheme, rhythm pattern etc..

Experiences with poetry writing can be included in all curriculum areas. Young people should engage in a variety of poetry writing activities from structured, formulaic verse to the creation of their own styles and forms as outlined in the following pages.

Concrete Poetry

In order to develop confidence in themselves as writers, students can begin by creating concrete poetry. In concrete poetry, the poem assumes the shape of the subject the poet is writing about, as shown in the example in the margin. The content of the poem may feature repetitive words or phrases that describe the selected topic or include a poem about the item itself.

Pattern Poetry

Pattern poetry enables students to experiment with words, explore language forms and use parallel structures. These structured verses provide young writers with a framework for expressing their ideas. Pattern poems do not have rhyming lines, but they do have patterns that makes them good models for students. The words, sounds and meaning have a particular form or shape. Pattern poetry can take many forms.

P eacefully beautiful
O ffended by pollution
N eeds cleaning up
D isrupted by wind.

Adam, Age 10

Acrostics

An acrostic is a form of pattern poetry that is especially easy to write. The title or topic of the poem appears in capital letters vertically on a page. The verses in the poem then begin with the first letter in each line as shown. Each line describes the topic in detail using single words or phrases.

Cinquains

A cinquain is another form of pattern poetry that students can create. A cinquain is a shape poem composed of five lines. The lines of the poem are based on either a word or syllable count, as demonstrated below and on the form on the following page.

By creating cinquain poems, young writers can examine literary devices, apply grammatical components and explore language functions in a meaningful way. Teachers can use these poetry writing experiences as opportunities to teach parts of speech (nouns, verbs, adjectives), vocabulary elements (synonyms), spelling conventions (syllables), diction (word choice) and the purposes of writing (to express thoughts, feelings, ideas etc.).

Creating cinquain poems also allows children to explore a chosen theme, such as the Environment, in detail.

Word-Based Cinquain

Beaver
Canadian symbol
Splashing Building Swimming
Lives in the forest
Animal

Adam, Age 10

Syllable-Based Cinquain

Winter
Windy Foggy
Ice skating freezing cold
Tobogganing in the cold snow
Snowman

Reena, Age 9

Haiku

A haiku is a form of Japanese poetry that usually describes an aspect of nature. When writing a haiku, the poet tries to capture a moment in time or convey a mood or feeling in a compelling way. This sophisticated form of poetry also follows a set pattern. It has three lines and seventeen syllables arranged in the following format:

Line 1: 5 syllables
Line 2: 7 syllables
Line 3: 5 syllables

Cinquain Poetry

Word-Based Cinquain

_____
(NOUN)

_____   _____
(ADJECTIVE)   (ADJECTIVE)

_____   _____   _____
(VERB)   (VERB)   (VERB)

_____ _____ _____ _____
(FOUR-WORD PHRASE)

_____
(SYNONYM)

Line 1:   one word for the title or topic (noun)
Line 2:   two words that describe the title or topic (adjectives)
Line 3:   three words to express action (verbs)
Line 4:   four-word phrase describing actions or feelings
Line 5:   one word that repeats the title or topic, creates a special effect or has the same
          meaning as the title or topic (synonym)

Syllable-Based Cinquain

_____
2 SYLLABLES

_____
4 SYLLABLES

_____
6 SYLLABLES

_____
8 SYLLABLES

_____
2 SYLLABLES

Line 1:   word(s) with a total of two syllables
Line 2:   words or phrases with a total of four syllables
Line 3:   words or phrases with a total of six syllables
Line 4:   words or phrases with a total of eight syllables
Line 5:   word(s) with a total of two syllables

As students use this structured form to express their ideas, they should consider the syllable count to produce a traditional haiku. As young poets polish their writing, they learn to control language and convey images with few words, as shown in the examples below.

> *A beautiful tree*
> *Basket filled with tasty fruit*
> *Good enough to eat.*
>
> Pasquale, Age 12

> *Leaves fall to the ground*
> *A ray of different colors*
> *Blanket for the earth*
>
> Adam, Age 10

Rhyming Poetry

Rhyming poetry is one of the most enjoyable forms of poetry for children. The delightful sounds of rhyme can be heard in nursery and schoolyard rhymes, music lyrics and greeting cards. Rhyme adds to the musical quality of a poem and gives it lasting appeal.

Writing rhyming poetry enables students to experiment with words and play with language to make it rhyme. Challenging young writers to express ideas through rhyme helps them make connections between the sounds of words and the letters that form them. Experimenting with words and letters can contribute to vocabulary development. The patterns of rhyming poems make them good models for students. There are many formats for rhyming poems.

Limericks
Students can develop an enjoyment for rhyming poetry through the humor and images of nonsense verse. Limericks are nonsense poems that tell a joke or funny story about a person, animal, place or another topic in the writer's imagination. A limerick consists of five lines organized in a specific rhyming and rhythmic pattern. The content, rhythm and rhyme scheme of a limerick are presented on the form on the following page.

Creating limerick poems challenges students to work with patterns and experiment with words in ways that rhyme. As children create nonsense poems, such as the ones shown below, they are able to explore aspects of a particular topic or theme in a humorous way.

> *There once was a man named Roose.*
> *Who traveled around on a goose*
> *One day in poor weather*
> *The goose lost his feathers*
> *Now the man rides around on a moose.*
>
> Kadeen, Age 10

Limericks

_____

_____

_____

_____

_____

Content

Line 1:   Introduces the subject or character
Line 2:   Includes an important detail about the subject or character
Lines 3 & 4: Describe an action or a situation that involves the subject or character
Line 5:   Completes the limerick with a surprising or unexpected ending that usually
              resolves the situation in a humorous way

Rhythm

Lines 1, 2 and 5 contain no more than nine syllables each (three beats)
Lines 3 and 4 contain no more than six syllables each (two beats)

Rhyme

The rhyme scheme is _a, a, b, b, a_
Lines 1, 2 and 5 rhyme
Lines 3 and 4 rhyme

There once was a fish in a pond
Who had hair that was blond
He once met a wizard
Who got bit by a lizard
Now the fish swims around with a wand

Adam, Age 10 and Pasquale, Age 12

Other Forms of Rhyming Poetry
Producing rhymes engages students in the playful use of language to entertain others. Creating rhymes can extend into other poetry experiences in the classroom and beyond. Students may wish to produce other types of rhyming poetry such as:

- Couplets;
- Quatrains;
- Schoolyard rhymes;
- Song lyrics;
- Greeting card verses.

Autobiographical Poems

Poetry is one of the most powerful forms of communication that writers can use to express their personal selves. Young people can find their voice, give shape to their thoughts and reveal aspects of themselves through poetry. By creating autobiographical poetry, children can express their identity from different dimensions and points of view.

Students can write their own autobiographical poems by selecting an object or abstract idea that both reflects their personality and relates to a particular topic or theme, such as the Environment. Students can then make comparisons, compose similes and attach human qualities to the object or idea they chose.

Using these conventions will enable young writers to depict their individual qualities and personal characteristics (moods, likes, dislikes etc.) in a metaphoric way. Likewise, by using stylistic devices like personification, comparisons and similes, young people can add depth to their poetry writing while growing in their own self awareness. Students can use these literary tools to create other forms of poetry too.

The following autobiographical poems were written by my students:

The Seasons

I am like the seasons
My moods are always changing
From the bright and happy summer
To the cold and angry winter storms.

Sometimes I am down
Like the falling leaves of autumn
And sometimes I am up
Like the blooming flowers of spring.

Bismattie, Age 11

Upinder, Age 9

I Am Like the Weather

Mad like a blizzard
Warm like the shining sun
Moving quickly like the blowing wind
Soft like white snow
Slippery like ice on cold days
Wet and lonely on rainy days.
Mad,
    warm,
        moving,
            soft,
                slippery,
                    wet,
                        lonely,
I am the weather wrapped up all in one.

Bena, Age 10

Contrast Poems

The world is filled with diverse images. As young people observe and reflect upon experiences and ideas, they may learn to examine life from different perspectives. Children can express their visions and impressions through poetry. Writing contrast poems enables young people to use sophisticated literary techniques like similes, metaphors, comparisons, contrasts, analogies and parallel structures to describe images vividly and create a special effect in their writing. These learning experiences can also be used to teach vocabulary and grammatical components.

To assist students in writing contrast poems around a particular topic or theme, such as the Environment:

- Generate a list of topics related to the theme (e.g., sun and moon, earth and sky, land and water etc.).
- Brainstorm synonyms and antonyms that can be used to describe the various topics.
- Ask students to write similes, metaphors and comparisons for the topic they selected.
- Have students organize their ideas using a parallel structure.

Creating contrast poetry related to a particular theme challenges young people to use sophisticated writing tools and complex forms to convey strong images, as illustrated in the examples below:

Earth
Heavy as rock
Hard like brick
Orbits around the sun
A source of roots
Land

Sky
Light as a feather
Soft like cotton
Leads up to heaven
A place for storms
Air

Adam, Age 10 and Pasquale, Age 12

Writing contrast poems also enables students to make connections between items that may at first seem different, but with closer observation and thought, can be strongly related. In the following examples my students compared images of War and Peace to aspects of the Environment:

War
A storm destroying everything in its way
A bull charging at its prey
Not stopping until it gets its victim
A lion defending its life.

Peace
A brightly colored rainbow
With a pot of gold at the end.
A bird singing and chirping
On a wonderful sunny day.

Ajay and Rajendra, Age 10

Free Verse Poems

Experiences with poetry can reach the inner core of children and inspire them to write from the heart about experiences and subjects that really matter to them. When students are not bound by restrictions on rhyme, number of verses, length of lines or other limitations of patterned, structured poetry, their ideas and emotions can emerge naturally and assume different sounds, images, shapes and formats.

Teachers should provide children with meaningful learning experiences that invite them to respond in poetic ways. Students can write free verse poetry in response to issues or situations they believe to be important. Young people should be encouraged to write poems rooted in personal experience or based on profound topics that evoke deep emotions. In order to encourage students to express themselves using this art form, poetry activities can be integrated throughout the curriculum.

Young people should also have the opportunity to create works of poetry related to a particular topic or theme. During a unit on the Environment, for example, my students studied the behavior of whales in their ocean community. The children were fascinated with the forms of communication used by whales in their habitat and wanted to try writing poems.

MY WISH

I Wish I was a bird

that could fly

And touch the sky

I wish I was a snow flake

that could come down very softly

Kiss the green grass very gently, and

cover the ground with my soft body.

Homyra Omar
11 years old
Room 126

Homyra, Age 11

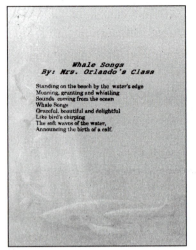

Grade Four Students

After reading the picture book *The Whales' Song* by D. Sheldon and G. Blythe to the class, the students brainstormed words to describe the sound of whale songs. Using a thesaurus, learners produced a list of synonyms for the words they generated. In word webs and concept maps, students recorded the names of places where whale songs could be heard. Through guided imagery and visualization, learners were able to envision themselves in these settings, experience the event on a sensory level, and later, describe their reactions and feelings to the sounds they heard in their imagination. The children then worked together as a large group to write a collective poem about whale songs that is illustrated in the margin.

Finally, the students were challenged to write their own poems about whale songs. Many young writers used literary tools like similes, metaphors and comparisons to express ideas in their free verse poems. The following poems were produced by my students:

On the Beach

Standing on the boat
Listening to sweet whale songs
Like bulls grunting
A wolf crying to the moon
Like thunder, the baby whale sings
A chirping bird calling out a melody to its mother.
Reminding me of my own mother
Singing to me when I was a baby.

Joshua, Age 9

Whales Singing

As I stand on the beach
I hear them sing softly.
Soft as the waves
Rolling on the rocks.
Like the wind blowing through the leaves.
So soft
So sweet
A peaceful sound
Such a lovely sound
Like a dream
The whales are singing
Happy songs for their loved ones.

Nadine, Age 9

Publishing Poetry in a Classroom Anthology

After writing poetry in a variety of forms, young people can share their poems with others by publishing them in an anthology. To do this:

- Provide an opportunity for students to revise and edit their poems with others before publishing them.

Bhumika, Age 9

- Hold writing conferences with the students that focus on vocabulary use, poetic format and content to ensure that the meaning of each poem is expressed as intended.
- Have students work with others to select the poems they want featured in the classroom collection, which will include poems on a particular topic or theme.
- Review the selections to ensure that all poems include the specific features of the formats used (e.g., number of lines, rhyming pattern etc.).
- Arrange for students to publish their work on the computer to give it a more professional look.
- Invite the children to create illustrations and other artwork to feature in the poetry collection.
- Have students work collaboratively to arrange the selections in the anthology (i.e., place the items in a particular order)
- Encourage students to produce a table of contents listing all items featured in the poetry collection.
- Ask students to design a cover for the anthology and bind the text.

Children's poetry collections can later be displayed in the classroom, resource centre, local library or a retail bookstore.

LEARNING CELEBRATION

Poetry Reading

Sharing work with audiences young and old alike can add to the enchantment and enjoyment of poetry. Invite children to present poems organized around a common topic or theme, such as the Environment, to others by holding a Poetry Reading. This literary event may feature the works of famous poets, as well as the children's work.

Prior to the celebration, have students select two or three favorite poems to share with others. Provide opportunities for children to practise reading their poems aloud using various techniques explored earlier in this chapter. Oral presentations can be accompanied with movement, music, slides and other visual displays. Readings can include solo, paired and choral performances. As a class, plan a schedule for these presentations.

Preparations for the literary event may also include designing invitations and distributing them to parents/guardians, administrators, famous poets, community members, and other teachers and students. Invite guests to bring their favorite poem related to the chosen theme to the celebration. Select a location for the Poetry Reading (classroom, library, auditorium) and create bulletin boards featuring "poet trees." As visitors arrive, have them post their poems on the branches. Display the thematic poetry anthology created by the class for others to enjoy.

Introduce the Poetry Reading session with a poem. Afterwards, students can present their solo, paired and choral readings in small or large groups. Invite guests to share their own poems with others. Distribute a poem or poems that participants can practise reading together. Conclude the celebration with a large group choral performance. Following the literary event, students may wish to write a thank-you verse to send to their guests.

EXTENSION ACTIVITIES

Encounters with poetry can be extended to include a variety of learning experiences where students experiment with other poetic forms, literary techniques and presentation tools that can enhance their enjoyment of poetry. For example, students may wish to:

- Compile their own personal poetry collections complete with published work by famous poets and their own poems.
- Create other forms of structured, patterned poetry and rhymes (e.g., diamantes, tanka, quatrains, couplets etc.).
- Write narrative poems, lyrical prose and free verse poetry on a range of personal topics, interests and learning experiences.
- Produce imitative, empathy, found and image poems.
- Apply other stylistic devices like irony, allusion, alliteration, puns, hyperboles etc. to their poetry writing.
- Respond to novels and other literary works through poetry.
- Write narrative poems and lyrical prose to explain story elements (characters, plot, setting etc.), personal reactions and interpretations of a literary text.
- Study and produce works of poetry based on popular themes, such as:

Childhood	Family	Friendship	Community
The Past	The Future	Celebrations	Sports
Mystery	Magic	Fantasy	Humor

- Include poetry writing as part of another genre study (e.g., write Five "W" poems during a study of the newspaper; publish narrative poems during a study of picture books).
- Present poems using multimedia tools (e.g., Kid Pix Slide Show).
- Recreate symbols and meanings of poems through visual arts projects (e.g., paper mâché, pastel drawings, collages etc.).
- Use poems as springboards for other creative activities in drama, dance and music (e.g., writing ballads).
- Study poems in children's collections (e.g., works compiled by David Booth), along with the life and works of famous poets (e.g., Dennis Lee).
- Publish a class poetry magazine featuring selections by famous poets and the students themselves.
- Enter a poetry writing competition or submit poems for commercial publication.
- Respond to learning experiences in social studies, science and other disciplines through poetry (i.e., present facts and concepts in poetic form).

Through authentic integration, children can experience classroom events through poetry throughout the year.

Over the years, poetry has become one of the most common art forms in society. As children, teenagers and adults, we delight in the magical verses of nursery rhymes, song lyrics, greeting cards and other forms of poetry that we encounter in our daily lives. Incorporating poetry into the classroom can lead to powerful and enjoyable learning experiences that actively engage children. Young people can examine issues, connect ideas, create meaning and extend their imaginations through poetry activities.

As students explore and create poems that relate to a particular topic or theme, they build essential knowledge and skills that can expand their vision and deepen their awareness of what it means to be human. By creating a climate that fosters poetic experiences, young people will learn to see life through a new dimension. Children will be able to listen, reflect, experience and respond to the world with new perspectives and understandings. Out of their growing enthusiasm for poetry may emerge a means of expressing who they are. These creative experiences may ignite a spark and inspire young people to write poetry throughout their lives.

CHAPTER FIVE

Investigating Non-Fiction

The construction of a newspaper that focuses on research and the past and present

Learning about the Past and Present can be intriguing for young people. Creating a newspaper about people, places and events both from history or the world today enables students to use non-fiction to conduct research in a meaningful context. By developing news publications based on this, or another interesting theme, learners will be able to build knowledge and language skills and share research information with others in a dynamic and attractive way.

INTRODUCING THE GENRE/THEME

Most of the reading people do throughout their lives is non-fiction. As they engage in daily activities, they encounter information in the advertisements, newspapers, recipes, manuals, reports and other factual content they read. The ability to read, understand and obtain information from non-fiction are important skills that young people need to develop in order to function in this information age. In school, students mostly encounter fiction resources and narrative texts that contain elements of story. Young readers need opportunities to read explanatory and informational texts in classrooms as well.

Using non-fiction resources, conducting research and writing explanatory texts can be challenging for students. Young people need to acquire research skills in a meaningful context by exploring topics that inspire them. History is filled with many fascinating periods marked by significant events, heroic tales, and famous people and places. Young people are often captivated by legendary periods in history and epic events of long ago. Learners can develop their inquiry skills by conducting non-fiction research about historical periods such as Pioneer Days, Medieval Times and Ancient Civilizations. Likewise, many students are eager to learn more about people, places, events and aspects of life in the world today. Classroom projects can also be based on important trends and events currently happening in the world.

By developing a unit based on a theme such as the "Past and Present," students can learn about history, modern events and other content areas in a personally relevant and interesting way. Likewise, many other topics and themes can be used successfully to engage students in the inquiry process.

Students benefit from integrated learning experiences that incorporate many skills and concepts. As described in this chapter, producing a news publication based on a specific topic or theme enables young people to:

- Develop skills in both media literacy and research;
- Understand different genres and sources of non-fiction;
- Explore characteristics of non-fiction and newspapers;
- Use explanatory texts to conduct research;
- Understand the topic being studied, including aspects of society (e.g., daily life) and systems of organization (e.g., economy, laws, government);
- Formulate questions to gain information;
- Gather information using different inquiry methods;
- Locate relevant information from a variety of sources;
- Read a variety of non-fiction materials;
- Develop reading comprehension strategies;
- Understand new vocabulary and concepts;
- Use appropriate terminology to present research findings;
- Compile information from a variety of sources;
- Communicate research findings using various media formats, written notes and descriptions;
- Write for complex purposes using a variety of forms;
- Analyze different news writing formats to determine features;
- Produce media texts using a variety of techniques and materials.

The learning activities in this chapter are designed to help students use non-fiction sources to conduct research on a topic related to a chosen theme, such as the "Past and Present." The teaching strategies provided will guide learners through a series of research steps to gather information and write various news items. Students will ultimately present their research findings in the form of a thematic newspaper and plan a learning celebration where their work can be shared at a Newspaper Release Press Party.

INTRODUCTORY ACTIVITIES

Exploring Types of Non-Fiction

Non-fiction materials are an excellent source of content when conducting research. Students should be encouraged to use a variety of materials to discover information, including print resources, information technology, primary and secondary sources, and other items of reference. As a class, brainstorm a list of non-fiction sources that can be used in the inquiry process, such as the one illustrated here.

Display samples of the various types of primary and secondary resources that can be used for research purposes. Have students identify the kinds of information contained in reference materials such as primary documents, artifacts, maps, illustrations and other types of resources.

Non-Fiction Sources

Primary Sources

- Personal interviews
- Surveys
- Letters
- Primary documents (original letters, diaries, journals, newspapers)
- Speeches
- Field research

Secondary Sources

Print Materials

- Non-fiction texts
- Reference books
- Trade books
- Encyclopedias
- Newspaper and magazine articles
- Works of historical fiction
- Catalogues and brochures
- Posters
- Newsletters
- Manuals
- Almanacs

Information Technology

- CD-Roms
- Internet sites
- E-mail correspondence
- Instructional videos
- Audiotapes
- Filmstrips
- Movies
- T.V. programs (documentaries)
- Radio broadcasts

Other

- Guest speakers
- Field trips
- Maps, atlases, globes
- Artifacts
- Artwork (sculptures, drawings, paintings)
- Illustrations
- Graphics (tables, graphs)

Examining the Newspaper

The Sections of a Newspaper

Understanding aspects of the medium is essential before students can produce their own newspaper. Before beginning the project, distribute copies of local newspapers and have students examine the different components in groups. As a class, make a list of the various sections and discuss the purpose of each. See the accompanying chart for an example.

The Sections of a Newspaper	
Section	**Purpose**
Front Section (feature articles)	To inform readers about leading news stories and important events that have happened around the city, country or globe.
Life	To feature news items related to different aspects of life, including health matters, education, religion etc..
Sports	To provide scores, updates, commentaries and recounts of different sporting events.
Fashion	To feature the work of different designers, collections and the latest trends in the area of fashion.
Entertainment	To guide readers through the world of entertainment by providing reviews, summaries and other information about films/movies, theatre, books, music etc..
Homes	To inform readers about the latest residential developments and provide tips on home improvement.
Business	To review developments in the world of commerce, business and the workplace, including stock market figures and innovative products on the market.
Automotive	To introduce new products in the automotive industry and other information related to the world of transportation (e.g., maintenance tips).
Classified	To feature want ads, job postings, items for sale and other classified information.
Travel	To guide readers in the world of travel by providing information about various destinations, airfares, departure dates, specials etc..
Editorials	To provide an opportunity for readers to express their opinions and offer commentaries on various subjects by writing their own letters and articles.
Other	To include special sections and inserts in a newspaper edition (e.g., commercial flyers).

Next, gather articles and other news clippings taken from the different sections of local newspapers. Ask the students to identify the sections where these news stories might be found and arrange them into categories. Encourage students to search through local newspapers and locate their own examples of news reports and other feature columns that can be found in each section. News clippings can later be arranged on a bulletin board outlining the various sections of a newspaper and the types of items found in each.

Types of News Items

Newspapers are filled with different types of news items. Most news articles are factual recounts and works of non-fiction. Apart from informational pieces, newspapers also contain other items produced for different purposes and intended for different audiences (e.g., instructions, explanations, persuasive pieces, word-play, narratives).

Before students can produce their own news reports and other news items, they need to be familiar with the various types of items featured in a newspaper. Ask students to revisit the different sections of the newspaper they observed previously and take note of the distinct items found in each. As a class, produce a list like the one shown here of the items featured in a typical newspaper.

Next, provide students with samples of different kinds of news items. Use file cards to record the names of each type of news item and distribute these to the students. Have them examine the samples and make a list of the characteristics of each type of news item. After examining the features of a classified ad, for instance, students may identify the following characteristics and list them on the file card:

- Job title;
- Job description;
- Education and experience;
- Qualifications required;
- Personal skills needed.

Students can later refer to these file cards when producing their own news items.

> **Types of News Items**
>
> - News articles, reports or stories
> - Classified/want ads
> - Advertisements
> - Letters (editorials, advice)
> - Announcements (births, deaths)
> - Weather forecasts
> - Tables, charts, graphs (sports scores, stock market)
> - Puzzles, games, comics
> - Reviews (books, movies)
> - Recipes and menus

CORE ACTIVITIES

Teaching Research Skills through Non-Fiction

Inquiry-based learning requires children to apply research skills when exploring non-fiction. Students need a variety of learning experiences in order to understand the steps in the inquiry process and develop effective methods of research and reporting.

As Stephanie Harvey illustrates in her book *Nonfiction Matters: Reading, Writing and Research in Grades 3-8*, teachers can assist students in acquiring the knowledge and skills required for non-fiction research by guiding them through the different stages of investigation and providing effective strategies for:

- Selecting topics;
- Developing questions;
- Collecting resources;
- Reading for content;
- Understanding non-fiction;
- Recording information and noting references;
- Organizing ideas;
- Presenting research.

Before engaging students in the inquiry process, it is important to teach them the fundamental research skills that follow.

Selecting Research Topics

Learning about topics like people, places, events and activities in a particular time period can arouse a sense of passion and wonder in young people that can promote non-fiction inquiry and independent research. Legendary stories and factual accounts of life during different time periods may inspire students to acquire knowledge and gain new insight about provocative topics related to the "Past and Present," or another chosen theme. Encourage students to investigate aspects of a theme by providing them with a comprehensive list of research topics, such as the one shown on this page, or have them brainstorm and select their own.

Provide students with time to review the research list and discuss the various topics that interest them. Have learners share what they know about the different inquiry topics and indicate what they still want to learn. Additional research topics can be generated from students' questions and content discussions.

Next, have students select their own research topics for non-fiction inquiry. Encourage them to review the list carefully, identify the topics they are interested in, select at least three of them and rate their preferences. Once students have made their final decisions, begin assigning research topics from the list provided or produced by the class. Keep a record of the topics that have been selected and indicate the name(s) of the student(s) who are responsible for each one on the research list. Assignments should be given to students in order of preference.

Learners who are interested in similar topics can examine different aspects of the same subject. For example, if students have decided to explore aspects of the Medieval time period, those who are interested in knighthood can examine: the stages of knighthood; the code of chivalry; the knighting ceremony; jousting tournaments; battles and conquests; armor and weapons; the life of a foot soldier or medieval man-at-arms etc..

If topics from the research list have already been assigned, offer additional suggestions of subjects learners may be interested in based on their background knowledge and personal interests. In order to engage students in successful research, the topic they choose to investigate

---

Sample Research Topics Related to a Particular Time Period

- Famous people
- Daily life
- The role of children in society
- The role of women in society
- The role of men in society
- Warfare and defense
- Armor and weapons
- Battles and conquests
- Banquets, feasts and festivals
- Trade fairs and marketplaces
- Occupations and the workplace
- Travel and explorers
- Transportation
- Entertainment
- Food and drink
- Education
- Recreation and sports
- Religion and belief systems
- Fashion and clothing
- Music and instruments
- Art and architecture
- Homes and dwellings
- Life in a town
- Life in a village
- Life in a city
- The political system (e.g., structure of government)
- The social system (e.g., hierarchy)
- The economy (e.g., trade and commerce)
- The legal/justice system (e.g., laws)
- Taxation
- Customs and traditions
- Medicine and disease
- Discoveries and inventions

should be one they know something about and are curious to know more about. Teachers may need to assist students who struggle with topic selection by generating ideas and presenting them with information they may find intriguing. Exploring trade books and content area discussions can also assist with topic selection.

Formulating Questions

Questions are an important part of the inquiry process. Once students have selected a topic, ask them to generate a list of questions that will guide them in their research. These questions should reflect aspects of the topic they are interested in finding out more about. Encourage students to produce as many questions as possible and record them in a comprehensive list as shown below. Afterwards, ask the children to share their inquiry questions with others.

Research Topic

The role of children in Medieval society

Questions I Wonder About

- What were children's responsibilities during the time period?
- What chores were boys and girls in charge of?
- Did children attend school during this time?
- What were boys and girls taught in school?
- What did children do in their spare time?
- What recreational activities and sports were boys and girls involved in?
- How did boys and girls contribute to the family?
- Were boys and girls treated equally?
- Did children have jobs outside of the home?
- Where did boys and girls spend their free time?
- How were the lives of children living in different areas (town, city) and parts of the world similar or different during this time?
- What was it like to be a child during this time period?
- Were any laws in place to protect children at this time?
- Were all children formally educated?
- How was the system of education during this time similar to or different from the system of education in our society?

Research questions can also be developed using a three-column chart, commonly known as a K-W-L chart, headed by *What I Know, What I Want to Know* and *What I Learned*. This graphic organizer, developed by Donna Ogle, enables learners to record background knowledge, research questions and information acquired throughout their investigations. Provide a model of how this chart can be used. In the example shown, information and research questions about King Arthur appear in a K-W-L chart as part of a study of the Middle Ages. The final column will be used to record research findings throughout the inquiry process.

K-W-L		
Topic: King Arthur		
What I Know	**What I Want to Know**	**What I Learned**
• King Arthur lived during Medieval Times. • There are many legends and stories written about his adventures. • He organized a group of knights known as the Knights of the Round Table. • He lived in Camelot. • Merlin, the Wizard, was his closest advisor. • He married Lady Guinevere. • He pulled a sword out of a stone and became King.	• Where was King Arthur born? When? • Who were his parents? • Did he have any brothers and sisters? • What were some adventures he was involved in? • When did he die? How? • How did he meet Merlin? Lady Guinevere? • Who were his enemies? • What deeds made him famous? • What was his childhood like? • How was he educated?	

Developing a Focus

In order to develop a focus for their research, students need to narrow down the questions they formulated into categories, headings or subtopics that will lead their investigation. Once these pivotal areas are determined, learners should arrange their questions under these general headings or subtopics as shown in the chart below. As students acquire information on these categories, their specific research questions may be addressed.

Categorizing Questions: Narrowing Down Research		
Topic: The role of children in Medieval society		
Subtopic: Education Related Questions:	**Subtopic:** Responsibilities Related Questions:	**Subtopic:** Pastimes Related Questions:
• Did children attend school during this time? • What were boys and girls taught in school? • Were all children formally educated? • How was the system of education during this time similar to or different from the system of education today?	• What were children's responsibilities during the time period? • What chores were boys and girls in charge of? • How did boys and girls contribute to the family? • Did children have jobs outside of the home?	• What did children do in their spare time? • What recreational activities and sports were boys and girls involved in? • Where did boys and girls spend their free time?

Teachers should guide students as they analyze their questions, categorize them and determine the subtopics that will lead them in their investigation. The pivotal areas that students have identified through this process will then become the focus for their research.

Gathering Information

Uncovering authentic information about research topics is the key to successful inquiry. Brainstorm a list of places where information can be located, including:

- Libraries;
- Bookstores;
- Museums;
- Public archives;
- Cultural institutions;
- Professional organizations;
- Community agencies;
- The Internet.

Consult the school librarian and other specialists (e.g., history teacher) to provide assistance for students as they search for resources and work through the inquiry process.

Arrange a visit to the school resource centre or local public library as a class. During the visit, ask students to locate a variety of non-fiction resources related to the theme being studied and produce a collection of reference materials that can be used throughout their research. Encourage them to search the shelves and other areas for books, magazines, encyclopedias, technology resources and other sources of non-fiction.

Assist learners in gathering authentic information by providing them with the following selection criteria:

- Look for key words in the title that relate to the topic being studied.
- Check the table of contents and index for a list of topics covered in the resource.
- Refer to the pages containing information on the selected topic and review the content (scan the main headings).
- Locate facts and details that answer key research questions related to the focus (subtopics).
- Consult other resources (at least three) for additional information on the topic.
- Check the dates of publication of all relevant materials to ensure that they are not outdated.
- Look for bias in reference materials (exclusion or misrepresentation of different groups) and disregard resources where bias has been detected.

After locating text resources from the library, students should gather information from other places of reference (e.g., museums, professional organizations, public archives etc.) using different inquiry methods. These might include:

- Conducting interviews;
- Developing surveys;
- Planning field trips;
- Attending workshops;
- Inviting guest speakers to discuss research topics.

Learners may require instruction and practice using some of these primary methods of inquiry to locate information. Research tools such as tape recorders, cameras, video cameras, clipboards and other useful resources may assist students in acquiring information.

Reading Non-Fiction

After students gather information from a variety of non-fiction sources, they must learn to read for content and select relevant facts and details on their research topic. Understanding informational texts can be challenging for young readers.

To assist students in developing an understanding of non-fiction, guide them in the following reading and comprehension strategies:

- Use prior knowledge and experiences to make sense of texts.
- Read sections of text (paragraphs, pages, chapters) dealing with the research topic for general understanding.
- Review questions related to the focus (subtopics) to determine what content in the text is important.
- Reread sections that contain relevant information.
- Look for headings, photographs, illustrations, examples, maps and charts dealing with the research topic.
- Select the main idea from the resource(s) used.
- Locate specific information, details and facts to support the main idea and subtopics.
- Ask questions throughout the reading process.

When students encounter challenging texts, encourage them to:

- Mark difficult passages with adhesive notes;
- Locate known words;
- Search for familiar information;
- Reread texts to confirm meaning;
- Use structural, context and visual cues to understand reading material;
- Monitor and self-correct their reading;
- Work with a teacher, partner or group of students;
- Share discoveries and findings with others in reading conferences.

Understanding New Vocabulary and Concepts

Reading non-fiction provides students with opportunities to develop their vocabulary and understand new concepts. As children learn about different topics, they may encounter unfamiliar terms throughout their research. In order to understand information on their inquiry topic, students need to clarify the meaning of unknown vocabulary.

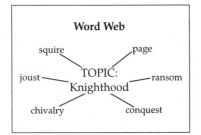

Word Web

squire   page

joust — TOPIC: — ransom
Knighthood

chivalry   conquest

To do this, begin by asking students to create a word web of terms associated with their topic. After brainstorming known terminology related to the subject they are investigating, have students record unfamiliar vocabulary encountered during the research process. For example, in exploring the topic of knighthood in a study of Medieval Times, the web might look like the one shown here.

Learners can then consult dictionaries and other vocabulary resources (e.g., thesaurus, speller etc.) to locate definitions and create a glossary of unknown terms as shown in the diagram below. By identifying related vocabulary associated with an unknown word, students are able to determine its possible meaning and later clarify it with a dictionary definition. Students should refer to this glossary of new vocabulary and word meanings throughout their research.

My Personal Glossary			
Unknown Word	Related Terms	Possible Meaning	Dictionary Definition

Recording Information

As students conduct research by exploring non-fiction resources using various information-gathering techniques, they should note important facts and details on their topic using different methods for record keeping. Encourage students to select the method for recording that they find most useful.

Review the skill of note-taking with the class by selecting a non-fiction passage about a research topic related to the chosen theme. After reading the excerpt aloud, have students identify the relevant facts and pertinent details about the subject described in the text. Guide them in the skill of note-taking by:

- Demonstrating the process of scanning information, marking the text and recording jot notes on an overhead projector using an unmarked copy of the passage read aloud.
- Recording only the most important ideas using your own words.
- Modeling the use of short phrases or sentence fragments (not complete sentences) when noting information.
- Using abbreviations, initials and other codes to increase efficiency of note-taking.
- Indenting information using asterisks, hyphens or bullets.
- Downplaying grammar, punctuation, spelling and handwriting at this stage of the inquiry process.

After providing a concrete example of the note-taking process, instruct students to use the same strategies for recording information on their topic. Guide them through this phase of research by monitoring their individual work. Remind students that information from trade books and other primary and secondary sources can be recorded using a variety of materials and formats, such as those outlined below.

Methods for Record Keeping

Research Notebook
Students can use a non-fiction notebook to record topic lists, research questions, references, resource locations, word webs, jot notes, outlines, rough drafts and other project work at various stages of the inquiry process.

File Cards
Students can use file cards to record factual content that answers each of their research questions. Index cards can also be used to note important information on the different subtopics. Specific facts and details can be written on individual note cards (use a separate card for each interesting fact) or single cards can be used for related information (use a larger index card to record factual content on each subtopic). Encourage students to use file boxes to store their index cards.

Notepads
Students can use coiled notepads to record information discovered during their research. Each page can be used to note specific questions, factual content, details or references.

Charts
Graphic organizers such as K-W-L charts can be used to record information that students learn about their topic throughout the inquiry process. In addition, teachers and students can develop their own column charts, or T-tables, to note information such as questions and answers, facts and opinions, familiar concepts and new ideas, subtopics and related details etc..

Lists
Students can compose lists at various stages of the research process. First, they can list research topics, questions and resources. As they acquire information, they can develop content lists on each of the subtopics and reference lists of the non-fiction texts used throughout their inquiry.

Computers
Students can use different computer programs and applications to record research information (questions, jot notes, outlines etc.) on individual laptop or desktop machines.

Noting References

As students engage in the inquiry process, they should note the non-fiction resources used to locate information throughout their research. Reference lists can take many forms, the most familiar being a bibliography. Teachers and librarians should provide students with basic skills on noting references by informing them of where to locate bibliographic information in various types of resources. This information includes:

- Author(s);
- Title;
- Place of publication;
- Publisher;
- Year of publication.

Afterwards, ask students to find and record the bibliographic information for each resource text they used, using one of the methods for record keeping previously discussed (e.g., index cards, recording sheets, computer database, research notebook page etc.).

The following provides examples of how bibliographic information for different sources of non-fiction can be recorded accurately. As more information becomes available from different sources, such as the Internet, teachers, librarians and students may need to develop other effective ways of noting research information.

Sample Outline
The Stages of Knighthood

- Requirements
  - had to be male
  - member of noble class
- Early childhood
  - raised by nurse
  - moved into home of knight to begin training
- Page
  - age: about 8
  - taught to ride horse
  - learned to use weapons
  - education (reading, writing)
- Squire
  - age: 15 or 16
  - dressed knights
  - served knight all meals
  - cared for horse
  - cleaned armor, weapons
  - learned to ride horse wearing armor
  - prepared for battle
- Knight
  - age: 19 or 20
  - before dubbing ceremony: fast and pray
  - ceremony (accolade)
  - feast
- Responsibilities
  - protect castle
  - battle and conquests
  - follow code of chivalry

Recording Bibliographic Information

Book

<u>Single Author:</u>

Beshore, G. *Science in Early Islamic Cultures*. New York: Franklin Watts, 1998.

<u>Two Authors:</u>

Delafosse, C., and J. Gallimard. *Cathedrals*. London: Moonlight Publishing, 1995.

Encyclopedia Article

Atkinson, R.J.C. "Stonehenge." *Encyclopedia Britannica*. Chicago, 1989. XXI, pp. 275-277.

Interview

Brown, Thomas, President, History and Social Science Foundation. Interview, April 10, 1999.

Organizing Content

After gathering information from a variety of resources and recording important facts and details about their topic, students need to organize content into a structural framework. There are various organizational strategies and styles that can be used to synthesize and record information prior to report writing. Some of these are described below.

Outline

As illustrated in the example, students can develop an outline for their report using subheadings, bullets and indentations. To prepare for this, learners should:

- Sort through research information;
- Locate jot notes on each of the subtopics;
- Use numbers, letters, colored highlighters or other codes to mark related information;
- Arrange jot notes under appropriate subheadings, listing important facts and details related to each subtopic;

- Develop additional subtopics for related information.

Teachers may wish to model this method of organizing content for their students.

Sequence Cards
Index cards containing research information can be organized according to subtopics. To do this, students should:

- Sort through the file cards;
- Arrange them into content groupings;
- Place each set of cards in chronological order;
- Use note cards as a guideline for recording information in sequence when writing their report.

The same method of organizing content can be used for information recorded on note pads.

Webs, Maps and Charts
Research notes can also be organized using different forms of graphic outlining. Graphic organizers such as webs, maps and charts can be used to sort information, develop subtopics and present supporting details. Students can structure information visually using webbed groupings, concept maps and column charts prior to report writing. Learners may wish to arrange content around pivotal areas of organization, such as research questions or subtopics, and include supporting details using graphic links, tables or other visual tools to connect ideas. In the following example, information about jousting tournaments that took place in the Middle Ages is arranged using a web format.

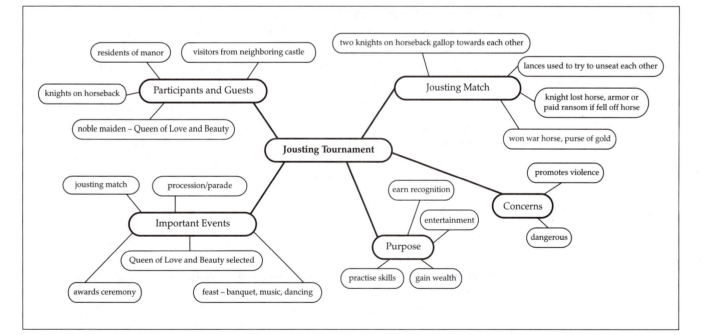

Presenting Research Findings through the Creation of News Items

Research findings can be presented in many ways. One way to present factual information is by producing a class newspaper organized on a common topic or theme such as a time period related to the "Past and Present." In addition to becoming familiar with another literary genre and exploring a chosen theme in more depth, creating a thematic news publication allows young people to write using a variety of formats. These might include news stories, recounts, instructions, explanations, persuasive writing, word-play and other explanatory texts. Before publishing a class newspaper, teachers should explore the features of different types of news writing with their students.

News Stories and Recounts

The pages of a newspaper are filled with feature articles and news stories about real people and events. These factual recounts retell an experience or incident in chronological order using clear, simple, accurate and concise language. News reports generally begin with a compelling introduction that attracts the reader's attention. Important events and information are then elaborated on and described sequentially. Details are often included to add interest. The news story usually ends with a well-crafted conclusion that summarizes the main features of the article. Factual content includes information that answers the 5W and H questions (Who? What? When? Where? Why? How?) essential to news reporting.

The Parts of a News Story
Before producing their own news stories based on a chosen theme, such as a time period related to the "Past and Present," students need to be familiar with the components of a news report. To do this, have students examine several articles from the main section of the newspaper and note similarities in writing style and format. As a class, make a list of the parts of a news story. These might include:

- Headline;
- Byline;
- News photo;
- Photo caption;
- Lead paragraph;
- Body;
- Conclusion.

To reinforce the information, cut out a series of headlines, bylines, photos, photo captions, lead paragraphs, body texts and conclusions from news stories in the main section of local newspapers. Distribute samples to the students and have them identify each part. Encourage students to collect their own newspaper clippings and display them on a bulletin board featuring the different labeled parts of a news story.

Ajit, Age 9

The Structure of News Stories

Like other forms of writing, news reports have a distinct structure or format. In order to help students understand this unique writing style, read several news articles from different local newspapers to the class and have students read their own news stories. Following each one, ask learners to identify the main events described in the article.

As a class, examine the headline and lead paragraph of several news stories and discuss the particular information revealed in these parts of the news report. Introduce students to the newspaper writing format known as the "inverted pyramid" illustrated on the following page, where information is arranged from most important to least important. Compare and contrast this form of writing to the structure of a narrative. Explain the importance of the 5W (Who? What? When? Where? Why?) and H (How?) questions in the organization of information on the inverted pyramid. Have students reread several news articles and select the information that answers the 5W and H questions in each of the stories.

To consolidate students' understanding of this distinct writing style, have them work in partners to deconstruct and reconstruct articles from local newspapers, using the inverted pyramid provided. First, ask each student to select a news report from the main section of a newspaper. Using a pair of scissors, have the student cut the article into separate parts and mix the components together. Next, have a partner arrange the elements (headlines, photo, captions, paragraphs etc.) in a logical sequence so the story follows the structure of the inverted pyramid and makes sense to the reader. Display the inverted pyramid on the bulletin board for future reference.

Preparing a Rough Draft of a News Story

After reviewing the inverted pyramid format for writing a news story and organizing their research notes using an organizer like the News Story Outline provided on page 111, ask students to write a rough copy of their newspaper article related to the chosen theme.

Model the process of news writing for the students by producing a sample recount with the class. Assist the students as they write their own news stories. The children in my class wrote intriguing news stories about famous people from the Middle Ages, important battles and conquests, innovative inventions developed during Medieval Times, along with many other fascinating topics related to this time period.

Persuasive Writing

Persuasive writing is writing that tries to sell a product or service, convince others of an idea or influence people to think in a certain way. Newspapers are filled with different forms of persuasive writing. Advertisements try to convince readers to buy products and services. Editorials, advice columns and reviews present arguments and opinions that try to sell ideas and beliefs. Teachers should provide students with opportunities to produce advertisements, editorials, advice columns, reviews and other types of persuasive writing that can be included in their class newspaper.

The Inverted Pyramid

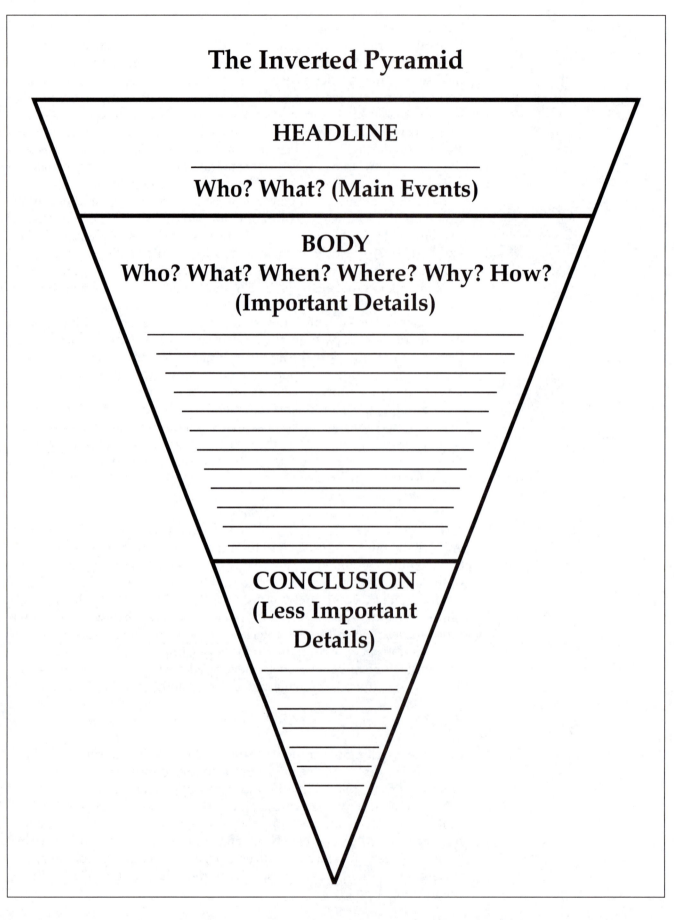

HEADLINE

Who? What? (Main Events)

BODY
Who? What? When? Where? Why? How?
(Important Details)

CONCLUSION
(Less Important
Details)

News Story Outline

Headline: _____

(Who? What?)

Byline: _____

Leading Paragraph/Introduction: _____

_____

_____

_____

Subtopic #1: _____

_____

_____

_____

Subtopic #2: _____

_____

_____

_____

Subtopic #3: _____

_____

_____

_____

Other Interesting Facts: _____

_____

_____

Conclusion: _____

_____

_____

Photo:

```
┌──────────────────────────────────────────────┐
│                                                │
│                                                │
│                                                │
│                                                │
│                                                │
│                                                │
└──────────────────────────────────────────────┘
```

Photo Caption: _____

Advertisements

Advertisements include forms of persuasive writing that attempt to sell a product or service. Newspapers are filled with various types of advertisements, including posters, flyers, classified ads, job listings, slogans and so on. As a class, examine the specific features of these different forms of writing. To do this:

- Select examples of various ads from local newspapers and distribute them to the students.
- Encourage the children to locate their own samples of different kinds of ads.
- Ask students to record the characteristics or features of the different forms of advertisements while working in groups.

Afterwards, encourage students to produce items for the class newspaper using at least one of the different forms listed above. To create a classified want ad, for instance, the students can do the following:

- Examine job postings and want ads from the classified section of local newspapers.
- Review the specific features of these news items.
- Brainstorm a list of occupations related to the chosen theme being studied.
- Investigate the duties and responsibilities of these different occupations.
- Determine the job qualifications, education and experience required for each.
- Write a classified want ad for their own class newspaper.

In my classroom, the students produced classified want ads for occupations people held in the Middle Ages (steward, minstrel, stone mason, jester, lady-in-waiting etc.). These job postings were later published in our Medieval newspaper.

In addition to classified want ads, the students created posters for the sale of products like armor, weapons and castles that were included in the class newspaper as well.

To create a poster advertisement, the students can do the following:

- Examine posters around the school and local community.
- Identify the characteristics of this form of advertisement (e.g., pictures, slogans, symbols etc.).
- Select a product, related to the chosen theme, that they wish to sell.
- Write a product description that explains the uses and special features of the item being sold.
- Create a slogan (i.e., short, catchy phrase) that summarizes the message of the poster and the product in a fun and interesting way.
- Use signs, symbols, pictures, color and a variety of print sizes to design a poster that features the product and related information.

By producing different types of ads, students will learn to experiment with language, convey different messages and present ideas using various styles to attract readers.

Nurse Wanted In The Castle

Hear Ye! Hear Ye! Nurse wanted in the castle to make food, prepare clothing and make beds for the noble children. The Lady must know how to cook food, weave and sew fabrics, lay out clothing and make beds neatly. She must have the skills to satisfy and discipline the children of the Noble family and must be neat when cleaning up. A reward of a room, food and 4 silver coins will be given. Please report to the castle drawbridge on February 11, 1172.

By:Santhy Rajah

Santhy, Age 9

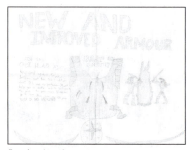

Jamie, Age 9

Letters to the Editor

Writing letters to the editor enables students to state their opinions and present their points of view on various topics and issues. Arguments or ideas are often expressed with supporting evidence and details. These steps can help prepare students for writing their own theme-related letters to the editor:

- Select examples of editorial articles and letters to the editor from local newspapers.
- Examine the features of these forms of persuasive writing as a class.
- Produce a list of criteria for writing letters to the editor.
- Brainstorm a variety of issues or topics that students may have strong opinions about (e.g., violence on television).
- Prepare to conduct a debate about a real issue or topic that the children are interested in (e.g., school routine).
- Challenge the students to present a case for or against a particular point of view, as illustrated in the chart below.
- Encourage them to gather information (including supporting evidence) and organize it before presenting their arguments during the debate.
- After the debate, reflect on the effective methods used to present the opposing arguments and the convincing details mentioned to support each case.

Learning to Take a Stand: Presenting Both Sides of a Case Topic or Issue: Violence in Tournaments	
Arguments For	*Supporting Details, Evidence, Facts and Examples*
• Entertains the audience	– draws large crowds – spectators cheer loudly
• Helps knights develop skills in warfare necessary for the battlefield	– forces participants to use their weapons skillfully to defend themselves – knights learn to fight on horseback
Arguments Against	*Supporting Details, Evidence, Facts and Examples*
• Dangerous	– participation in tournaments may result in serious injury and death
• Opposes laws of conduct in society	– sets inappropriate example for re-solving conflicts – acts of violence are against the law in society
• Sets negative example for others	– members of society may imitate violent behavior and use weap-ons on others

Once the students are ready to try writing a letter to the editor:

- Produce a list of potential topics that are related to the chosen theme for the class newspaper.
- Ask students to select a topic that is of interest to them and compose arguments for and against both points of view regarding the same issue.
- Challenge learners to provide evidence, details, facts and examples that support both sides of the argument.
- Have students locate, organize and record relevant information on the topic in a chart or another graphic form.
- Ask the children to write a letter to the editor expressing their personal opinions on the issue.

Dear Editor,

My name is AJIT RAI. I'm writing to you to explain why violence should not be part of tournaments. Although it is entertaining, violence can harm knights. The weapons are very dangerous and sharp. When a knight loses a tournament, he loses his armour, so he is left without any protection. People can still enjoy watching knights wearing armour and weapons. People who come to watch tournaments can get food and still be entertained. So please stop the violence in tournaments.

Sincerely,
AJIT

Teachers should model writing a case for or against a particular viewpoint by producing a letter to the editor with the class. Characteristics of letter writing may need to be reviewed.

During our unit on the Middle Ages, the students and I discussed aspects of Medieval life and raised issues about common practices of long ago such as violence in tournaments and the lack of education for peasant children. These controversial practices and issues provided opportunities for both debates and the writing of letters to the editor that were included in our class newspaper.

Instructions and Explanations

Instructions and explanations are forms of writing that describe how to do something and demonstrate how things work. People encounter this form of non-fiction in their daily life when they read manuals, guides, game rules, instructions, diagrams, menus and recipes. Newspapers frequently feature a variety of examples of instructions and explanations.

As a class, examine the characteristics of these different types of writing. To do this:

- Encourage students to collect and review examples of instructions and explanations in their everyday life (e.g., recipe books, instruction booklets, operating manuals, science experiments etc.).

- Have students identify the steps within the instructions and explanations they have collected.
- Ask the children to provide instructions or explanations for activities and events they participate in daily (e.g., brushing their teeth, playing a schoolyard game, preparing breakfast etc.).
- Encourage the students to record these procedures in detail.
- Examine the methods described by the students closely.
- Invite volunteers to follow the steps provided by peers.
- Discuss the importance of sequencing and accuracy when writing instructions and explanations.

Encourage students to include these forms of writing in their class newspaper. Writing instructions and explanations such as menus and recipes enables students to experiment with language in a variety of ways. Learners develop their descriptive writing skills as they convey details in a concise, sequential and accurate way. Menus and recipes make enticing additions to a class newspaper. For example, after reading the story *A Medieval Feast* by Aliki to the class, my students were asked to create a menu of Medieval foods for the class newspaper.

Other Forms of News Writing

Apart from recounts, persuasive pieces and procedures, newspapers contain many other forms of writing. Encourage students to create additional items for the class newspaper using different writing formats. For example:

- Transcripts or summaries of interviews;
- Timetables, daily schedules;
- Entertainment guides;
- Community announcements (births, deaths, weddings etc.);
- Tables, charts, graphs (e.g., sports scores);
- Comics, puzzles and other forms of word-play;
- Advice columns;
- Reviews.

Putting It All Together — Going to Press

Creating a thematic newspaper involves students in various stages of the writing process and the production of a publication. By this stage of the project, students have gathered research information, organized the content and prepared a first draft of their news item. At this point they are ready to edit and publish their news items for a newspaper that can be shared with others.

Editing News Items

When producing a news publication, journalists are required to present articles and other news items to an editor for review before going to press. To give them experience with this process, encourage young writers to edit and revise their work both individually and with peers once all news stories and feature columns are complete.

Balraj, Age 9

Guidelines for revision can be provided to students. For example, during peer conferences, learners should review the content of news items and offer suggestions about:

- Presenting concepts;
- Developing ideas;
- Improving language;
- Clarifying content;
- Ensuring accuracy.

Student editors may recommend the following changes to news items:

- Adding content;
- Deleting unrelated information;
- Reorganizing the structure of news items (e.g., moving sections of text);
- Adjusting the style and presentation of news items.

Peer editors should also proofread news reports and check:

- Spelling;
- Grammar;
- Punctuation;
- Capitalization;
- Sentence variety.

Later, the teacher, acting as the editor-in-chief, should hold a writing conference with each student and do a final check on news articles for the above-mentioned criteria before final drafts are published. Once revisions are made and items are proofread, individual news items can be published.

Publishing News Items

Raphael, Age 9

News items created from non-fiction research can be published using different technical formats and presentation tools. For example, with the use of word-processing programs students can easily type their news items, which can later be cut and paste into the format of a newspaper. Desktop publishing programs, such as ClarisWorks® or QuarkXPress®, allow students to print reports and feature articles into a news column format automatically. Multimedia software packages such as Hyperstudio® and KidPix Slide Show® are also well-suited for developing a class newspaper.

Alinthia, Age 9

A digital camera provides a useful tool for capturing photographs of field trips, guest speakers, artifacts, special events and other related items that can be scanned into the news publication. Photos and photo captions can be produced using different software draw programs as well.

Designing a Layout

Newspapers present individual items in a variety of different ways. Invite students to examine local newspapers for different models for presenting items. Following that, review the various sections of a newspaper as a class. Ask students to explore each section and identify the unique textual and visual features of the layouts that are included.

After compiling the feature articles and other items for their own class newspaper, have the students determine which section each item they created should appear in (e.g., a report on Medieval inventions might appear in the business section). As a class, decide on the order in which items are to appear in the newspaper. To do this, the students should consider the newsworthiness of each item. The front page news, for example, should include the most important and influential news items. Following the front section, the students can place news items that belong to the other sections of the newspaper and decide on the order of these sections by consulting local newspapers for ideas.

Once students have determined where items are to be located and have arranged the sections in sequence, they can design sample layouts manually or on the computer. Students should consider the following criteria when designing their layout presentation:

- The size of news items;
- The shape of news items;
- Using visual items to break up text (e.g., photos);
- Including advertisements among news articles;
- Using a variety of print sizes and fonts to make information stand out.

Feature columns, photos, photo captions and other necessary items (i.e., title of the newspaper, name of each section, publication date) should all be included in the section layouts.

By transferring all published news items onto a class disk, articles can be arranged into the sections of the newspaper in an attractive and logical way using a desktop publishing program. Afterwards, copies of the final newspaper can be made for distribution.

LEARNING CELEBRATION

Newspaper Release Press Party

Developing a successful thematic newspaper through non-fiction research can be a challenging endeavor for students that requires continuing effort, interest and commitment. Once the final news publication is complete, students should have the opportunity to share this enormous accomplishment with others. As a class, plan a Newspaper Release Press Party and invite guests (parents, administrators, other teachers and students) to the event.

Prior to the celebration, have students announce the publication of the newspaper over the public broadcast system and visit neighboring classes with a circulating copy. As a class, construct a newsstand where newspaper editions can be displayed.

During the event, conduct a formal presentation where the final publication can be revealed to guests. Throughout the celebration, students can share their experiences of doing non-fiction research, preparing news items and publishing the newspaper. The children should also have an opportunity to read their news stories to others.

Copies of the news publication can then be distributed to guests to read independently. At the end of the party, awards can be distributed to students honoring them for their successful achievements in non-fiction research and news writing/publication.

EXTENSION ACTIVITIES

There are a wide range of possibilities for students to use non-fiction research and various forms of writing to produce integrated learning projects. Developing a class newspaper is just one method of presenting research information on a common topic or theme.

Other alternatives include:

- Preparing oral presentations on the research topic for the class.
- Using the jigsaw method to learn about different aspects of a topic from a variety of sources and reporting findings to others.
- Creating a gallery or museum exhibit featuring artifacts, primary resources and other items related to the topic being studied.
- Designing a trivia game complete with a game board, instructions, playing pieces and trivia questions about the topic being explored.
- Creating newspapers, magazines, commercials, documentaries, video diaries, journals, photo essays and other forms of media around a variety of topics or themes (e.g., Life in the 21st Century: A Futuristic Look at the New Millennium).
- Producing multimedia projects about particular topics or themes, including magazine editions, videos, television commercials, Internet sites etc..
- Conducting research on a variety of topics or themes and presenting findings using various genres and writing formats, such as poetry collections, short story anthologies, informational picture books, works of historical fiction, primary documents (journals, diaries, letters, speeches, scrapbooks), brochures, catalogues and essays.

As people go about their daily lives, they encounter many works of non-fiction. Newspapers, for example, are part of the fabric of society, recounting events that happen to people in the surrounding community, nation and around the world. This and other forms of writing have become important means of communication in the information and electronic age in which we live.

Young people require experiences in both using and producing works of non-fiction. Inquiry-based learning through non-fiction research helps students build knowledge and language skills in a meaningful context. Publishing a thematic newspaper allows young people to use non-fiction for authentic purposes and to present research information in a genre that represents an authentic non-fiction format. Exploring and developing knowledge and skills in an integrated way helps learners understand the characteristics of both non-fiction and newspapers.

Teachers can create an environment for successful inquiry by developing integrated learning experiences around central themes, providing resources on compelling topics and inviting students to raise questions about people, places, events and issues that intrigue them. When young people are inspired by a sense of wonder, they are motivated towards further inquiry that can lead to greater knowledge, deeper learning and independent thinking.

CHAPTER SIX

Recounting Oral Stories

Storytelling that celebrates literature and the cultures of the world

At the beginning of each school year, I call my students together to listen to Knots on a Counting Rope *by Bill Martin Jr. and John Archambault. The story recounts the birth and naming ceremony of a young native boy as originally told by his grandfather. Afterwards, I invite my students to share stories of how they received their names. I listen with awe as some describe how religious books and national leaders played a part in their own "naming ceremony." As each story is told, each student ties a knot on a piece of string that slowly evolves into our own "counting rope." This ritual helps build a sense of community in my classroom — an atmosphere essential for storytelling.*

In observing children, it is plain to see that they are natural storytellers who enjoy the excitement, creativity and fun of listening to and telling stories. In addition to allowing students to build and review a range of language skills and knowledge, storytelling can also foster a sense of community and create an atmosphere where participants feel part of a global village. This makes the choice of Multiculturalism an ideal theme for celebrating a world of stories from novels and picture books to myths, legends, poetry, non-fiction stories and many more literary genres that are rooted in a variety of cultures.

INTRODUCING THE GENRE/THEME

The Culture of Storytelling

Storytelling is a traditional art form that is world renowned. This ancient ritual comes from a folk heritage based on shared narratives rather than written language. Many cultures from around the world are rooted in this oral tradition. Classrooms today are filled with students from diverse backgrounds. In the lives of these children, stories play an important part in their family history, relationships and life experiences. These children have a wealth of stories to share with others, making the theme of Multiculturalism an appropriate one to explore while engaging in storytelling.

Multicultural tales deal with general truths and human emotions that relate to us all. These stories are filled with archetypical characters with common personal traits who deal with basic moral issues familiar to people from around the world. Throughout history groups have told stories to entertain and preserve their cultural identity. Through stories and storytelling, people have been able to pass down beliefs, customs, traditions, laws and history from one generation to another.

Many of the stories told today are contemporary adaptations of original tales from long ago. Most folk tales, fairy tales, fables, myths and legends from the past have been preserved and adapted for present times. Although Multiculturalism works well as a theme for examining oral stories, other themes may be used just as effectively to teach the art of storytelling in the classroom.

The Art of Storytelling

As years pass, this oral art form is gaining a wider audience because of its universal appeal. As Marsh Cassady explains in his book *Storytelling: Step by Step*, "The purpose of storytelling, like any other art form, is to entertain, to present knowledge, to teach behavior and morals," as well as to inform and to explain.

Storytelling today is becoming a vibrant, living art that provides an aesthetic experience and has lasting appeal. As our lives unfold, many stories evolve from our personal experiences, family histories and encounters with literature. Stories come to us from many sources, including those shown on this page. Adults and children alike enjoy sharing tales with different audiences in various settings in our day-to-day encounters. Telling stories is a natural part of our lives and our relationships with others.

In recent years, there has been a resurgence of interest in storytelling as an art form. There is a profound difference between oral stories and those that appear in books, magazines or fiction anthologies. As Cassady points out, in storytelling the art occurs in the presentation. The storyteller conveys the excitement, drama and mystery of the story through the spoken word. Drawing on his/her creative imagination and a degree of skill, the storyteller gives life, color and feeling to the characters and the story as it is being told. The storyteller's face, voice, body, personality and background are tools he/she uses to convey the meaning, mood and actions of the story. Meanwhile, the listener creates the story in his/her mind. He/she forms the images and mental pictures as the tale unravels. Both the storyteller and the listener recreate the story each in his/her personal way using a variety of skills and knowledge. The art of storytelling is the interplay of the three essential elements described above and shown below: the story, the storyteller and the listener (or the audience).

Sources of Stories

- Life experiences
- Personal histories
- Family stories
- Fairy tales
- Legends and myths
- Fables and animal tales
- Tall tales
- Fortune stories
- Wishing tales
- Science fiction
- Supernatural stories
- Mystery stories
- Fantasy tales
- Contemporary tales

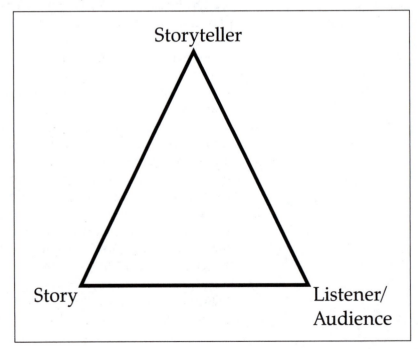

As I listen to and observe children engaging in the magic of storytelling, I see the rewards it brings to its participants — young and old alike. Storytelling can:

- Expand knowledge of literary genres, story structure and aspects of culture;
- Build language skills, including:
  - developing listening skills;
  - improving listening comprehension;
  - developing oral language skills (e.g., vocal techniques);
  - improving speaking ability (e.g., fluency);
  - developing oral presentation skills;
  - developing reading skills (e.g., sequencing, predicting, inferences);
  - improving reading comprehension;
  - understanding literary elements (e.g., plot, setting);
  - building vocabulary;
  - developing writing skills by providing models;
- Stimulate the imagination and creative thinking;
- Instill a love for language and enjoyment of literature;
- Develop an appreciation for other cultures;
- Build confidence and self-esteem.

The children in my classroom have gained a sense of self-worth in their ability to share stories with their peers. Many of them come from places like Africa, the Caribbean and India, all of which are rooted in this oral tradition. For these students, storytelling provides a familiar forum for telling tales and making literary connections. Storytelling enables them to feel successful using language in ways that both informs and entertains. At the same time, this experience gives validity and dignity to their languages and cultural experiences. Even the shyest child or ESL learner has been able to participate in our storytelling sessions and everyone has found the acceptance of both self and story a rewarding experience.

By engaging in the storytelling activities outlined in this chapter, students will have an opportunity to listen to stories read aloud, choose stories to tell, create story maps to assist in the retelling and share stories with others in an engaging way at a Storytelling Festival based on a theme such as Multiculturalism.

Introducing Storytelling

To introduce storytelling, begin by having children share personal experiences in the classroom. At the start of the school year, ask students to bring in a special object from home and explain its importance to their peers. Assign a personal scrapbook project or autobiography that motivates learners to tell stories about embarrassing moments and favorite childhood memories. Have students create personal timelines and present them to the class by relating family histories and cultural experiences. After sharing stories from their own lives, students will be ready to explore stories from literature and the outside world.

To move from the child's world of experience out into the wider world, involve the class in a variety of literary activities rooted in the story experience. For example, invite students to retell stories they have read from different characters' point of view or interview characters in role. Or, while listening to a story being read aloud, encourage children to use their imagination to visualize the story and later discuss the mental images they created.

Experiences in drama that require students to work individually and with others are particularly helpful for preparing them for storytelling performances that involve an audience. Provide opportunities for students to participate in such drama activities as:

- Awareness games;
- Improvisation;
- Role-play;
- Movement activities;
- Mime;
- Choral reading/speaking;
- Story drama.

There are an endless number of other ways to introduce students to storytelling and to encourage them to participate in this traditional art form. Students may become involved in literary activities, including:

- Reading stories aloud to develop fluency and expression;
- Listening to stories on tape and visualizing the elements;
- Engaging in stories that involve audience participation;
- Using prompts like story starters to develop cooperative stories;
- Creating illustrated retellings using different art mediums (e.g., mural);
- Developing oral stories based on wordless picture books;
- Using props such as flannel/felt boards, puppets or costumes to retell familiar stories from literature;
- Describing story elements (e.g., characters, setting etc.) orally following a read-aloud experience;
- Participating in group retellings after listening to a story.

Creating the Environment

The environment needs to be conducive to storytelling. Time, space and resources are essential. A designated area (in the classroom, school library etc.) should be established as the magical setting for storytelling to take place. For example, you may wish to have your students create a Storytelling Corner, complete with a rocking chair, rug, treasure chest, collection of books, and other ritual props like a story candle and a talking stick. Explain that each of these items is endowed with special importance and can be used by children and adult tellers only when a story is being told.

The environment may be further enriched with a display of interesting objects based on the chosen theme that can be used to generate storytelling ideas. Invite students to bring in items such as toys, games, crafts and artifacts from home that can appear in a teller's gallery or classroom museum. Encourage students to locate folk music or instruments from around the world that can be used to enhance the literary experience. These sounds may mark the beginning of a storytelling session or introduce a new tale.

Have the children make ritual props such as story hats and story sticks that can be used during storytelling presentations. For example, an elaborate story hat may feature unique designs and symbols from children's favorite narratives that can be worn by the storyteller. A decorative story stick embellished with colorful beads, textured fabrics and other craft items can be held by the storyteller. These objects add to the intimate warmth of the storytelling environment and help create an atmosphere of enchantment. The presence of folk music, ethnic crafts and cultural artifacts helps to invoke a sense of global community as well. Other items may appear at the Storytelling Corner to reflect the chosen theme.

CORE ACTIVITIES

Listening to Stories

Guidelines for Active Listening

- Establish close proximity to the storyteller (e.g., sit together as a group at the Storytelling Corner).
- Maintain eye contact with the storyteller.
- Avoid distractions (by others and objects).
- Refrain from discussion.
- Use your imagination to visualize aspects of the story (e.g., characters, setting) as these literary elements are being described by the storyteller.
- Focus on the events of the story as they unravel.
- Participate actively in parts of the story that require audience involvement (e.g., call and response, chiming in).
- Examine the techniques used by the storyteller during the presentation.

In order to become comfortable with storytelling, children should be immersed in stories and have endless opportunities to listen to narratives shared orally. Listening to others tell stories provides students with examples to follow. As Marion Virginia Ralston explains in her book *An Exchange of Gifts: A Storytelling Handbook,* children often model the language used by a storyteller when they tell tales of their own.

Invite professional storytellers and other guests like community members, librarians, older students and administrative staff to the classroom to tell stories to the students. Many professional storytellers are available through residency programs. In schools where community outreach programs do not exist, teachers may wish to learn to tell stories themselves to share with their students. Prior to the visits, review the active listening skills required by students during a storytelling presentation. Some of these are outlined on this page.

Following a storytelling event, discuss the various styles and techniques employed by the various storytellers during their presentations. Encourage learners to respond to the stories through creative drama, improvisation, music, visual arts and critical reflection. Students can create a tableau to depict an important scene or retell the story from a different character's point of view. Children can also select appropriate music to accompany the narrative or recreate powerful images from the story by designing a mural or other work of art.

One way of getting students to reflect on these literary experiences is to have them keep a storytelling journal where they can record their responses to tales told aloud, write critiques, extend the story or illustrate favorite parts. Advertisements, posters and bulletin board displays can also be created following a story. These, along with many other experiences, prepare children for their own telling.

Finding a Story to Tell

Stories come to us from a variety of sources, ranging from personal life experiences to traditional folklore. Before selecting a story for oral sharing, it is important to recognize the elements of a good story. After listening to narratives told from a variety of sources, students can develop their own criteria for recognizing a good story. A good story may include:

- Memorable characters;
- An exciting plot;
- A descriptive setting;
- Expressive vocabulary;
- Elements of suspense or mystery;
- A sense of humor;
- A high climax;
- Interesting details;
- An alternative ending.

Various authors point out appealing elements that make certain types of stories suitable for telling. In her book *The Way of the Storyteller*, Ruth Sawyer suggests that folktales, fairy tales, myths, legends and fables are the easiest to tell because of their oral structure. According to Ralston, the two major criteria for selecting stories are "minimum plot and maximum action." In these stories that usually depend upon action rather then description, the narrative begins quickly, moves sequentially towards a climax, and leads to a fast and logical conclusion. For Kerry Mallan, a good story has a quick beginning, an action-filled plot, an explosive climax, a limited number of characters, a repetitive language pattern and a satisfying ending. As Eileen H. Colwell points out in her book *Storytelling*, a good story should "inspire laughter and tears, bring home virtues of courage, kindness, loyalty and compassion, portray the ever-present struggle between good and evil, and touch the depths of human and spiritual experience."

Students should use the criteria they have developed to select a story of their own to tell that relates to the storytelling theme. If using the theme of Multiculturalism, encourage students to choose one from their ethnic background(s) or personal experience. Since many children come from a culture rooted in this oral tradition, they may already be familiar with stories from their childhood or ethnic heritage suitable for retelling (e.g., the popular tales of Anansi). Alternatively, suggest that children interview family or community members for a story from their ethnic background or a culture that interests them.

To assist the students with story selection, it is also important to provide the class with an array of stories suitable for retelling, including novels, picture books, myths, legends, folk tales, fables, poetry and non-fiction stories all organized around the chosen theme. Provide

<table>
<tr><td>

Methods for Learning to Tell a Story

- Read the story several times.
- Make an outline or story map.
- Learn the plot (main events).
- Develop a sense of the characters through role-play, writing-in-role etc..
- Gain an understanding of the characters' dilemmas and problems through discussion with others.
- Establish the setting by recreating an important scene visually or artistically.
- Analyze the story in detail.
- Make note of repetitive phrases.
- Visualize the story.
- Tell parts of the story aloud.
- Add gestures, change your voice, use props.
- Prepare a good introduction and conclusion.
- Practise the entire story aloud by timing it, tape recording it, telling it to others or retelling it in front of a mirror.

</td><td>

learners with the opportunity to review the selection of literature available.

To enhance a theme such as Multiculturalism, a collection of multicultural stories from around the world, such as those listed at the end of the book, can be available in the classroom. Introduce students to these reading materials by providing a brief summary of each item in the collection, including the country of origin and type of genre (e.g., legend, myth etc.). For children who wish to choose their story from this particular collection, guide them in their selection by suggesting that they choose a story based on their own ethnic heritage or another world culture that interests them.

Regardless of the theme organizing the learning, students should read several stories before deciding on the one they want to share with others. It is important that the children each select a different story to tell so that different aspects of the theme and various literary genres are represented. For the theme of Multiculturalism, for example, stories should reflect a variety of world cultures. This allows children to see that many folk tales, fairy tales, myths, legends and fables from around the world deal with similar themes, issues or characters.

Learners may also wish to select parallel versions of the same story to share (e.g., Cinderella). These stories can later be compared with similar traditional tales from other parts of the world or contemporary narratives with the same archetypes. After selecting a story that relates to the chosen theme, the students are ready to learn to tell their stories.

Learning to Tell a Story

Every storyteller has a unique way of developing his or her art. The techniques that can be used to remember and tell a story are endless. As a class, discuss effective ways of learning to tell a story. Afterwards, provide the students with a list of the methods they produced, along with other suggestions that may be helpful, as shown on this page.

Story Mapping

Story mapping is an effective tool that can be used to remember the parts of a narrative after first reading it several times. Students can then produce storywebs, storyboards, storycards and other types of story mapping diagrams that assist in the retelling, as shown on the following page.

In each of these graphic organizers, the main events, characters, settings, problems and key phrases of the story are recorded, illustrated and arranged in sequence using a format the learner is comfortable with. Students may select from the visual models provided or develop one of their own. This tool can then be used to guide them as they retell their narrative.

Practising Their Story

Before students share their narratives with a wider audience, they should practise telling their stories to their fellow peers. First, have children work in pairs listening to and telling their stories to one

</td></tr>
</table>

Nichole, Age 11

Story Mapping

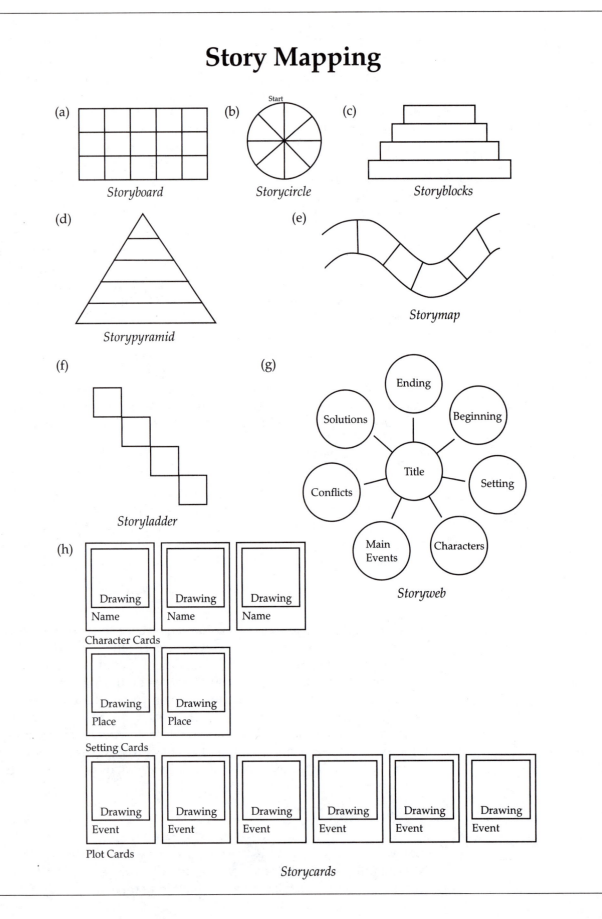

(a) Storyboard

(b) Storycircle

(c) Storyblocks

(d) Storypyramid

(e) Storymap

(f) Storyladder

(g) Storyweb

Ending · Beginning · Solutions · Setting · Title · Conflicts · Characters · Main Events

(h)

Drawing / Name

Drawing / Name

Drawing / Name

Character Cards

Drawing / Place

Drawing / Place

Setting Cards

Drawing / Event

Drawing / Event

Drawing / Event

Drawing / Event

Drawing / Event

Drawing / Event

Plot Cards

Storycards

another, referring to their maps when necessary. Pairs of students may then come together to form smaller groups where children can take turns sharing their stories with other members of the class. Encourage listeners to make suggestions on how the use of voice, facial expressions, eye contact, gestures and movement can be used effectively during the retelling.

While the children are practising their stories with others, invite individual students to make tape recordings of the stories they selected. Have each student play back the recording, noting the following items:

- The length of time required to tell the story;
- Vocal techniques that need to be developed (e.g., change of voice, fluency, clarity etc.);
- Parts of the story that required more practice;
- Specific elements of the story that need to be memorized or reviewed (e.g., repetitive phrase, important event);
- General improvements to be made before performing in front of an audience.

In addition to working with others and preparing an audio tape, students may practise the entire story aloud by retelling it in front of a mirror or producing a video tape of their performance. These strategies will assist beginning storytellers with the development of other techniques (e.g., facial expressions, gestures and movements) that might enhance the story presentation. Engaging in such experiences can help the story evolve into an art form that can be appreciated and enjoyed by others.

LEARNING CELEBRATION

Storytelling Festival

Once learners have had an opportunity to select and prepare their stories, they may be ready to share them with a wider audience in an oral presentation. Have the students, themselves, establish the storytelling schedule so they can present their stories when they feel they are ready. It is important to establish a classroom climate that is both accepting and non-threatening so that all learners feel comfortable sharing their stories with the class. Encourage audience members to compliment the student storytellers on their appropriate selections, interesting recounts, and effective use of voice and expression. Remind participants to be considerate and fair when offering additional suggestions on how learners can improve their individual techniques. The children will respond positively to constructive criticism when it is coupled with praise. Learners may take people's suggestions seriously when they see themselves as storytellers who want to master their art.

Once all the students have shared their stories with the class, plan a storytelling festival or oral literacy celebration based on the chosen theme. Learners can create story sticks, design "storyteller" hats, make decorations and write invitations. Include professional storytellers, community members, parents, administrators and students from other classes in the event. Select a setting for the festival and arrange storytelling stations filled with ritual props like chairs, blankets, candles and telling sticks.

During the celebration, the students can share their story selections as visitors gather and listen to individual tales or wander the room making their way from one station to another. Later, the guests themselves can be invited to share stories from their own cultural background or personal histories.

Extending the Story Experience

After children have shared their stories with others and listened to many tales told aloud, they can participate in related activities that extend the art experience. Following the festival, participants can visit local schools or community agencies to tell their stories and share their art. Articles and reviews can be written for a class newsletter, school newspaper or local community publication. These are just some of the experiences that can strengthen the students' involvement with the stories told aloud. The accompanying chart outlines some additional ideas.

Teachers and students can also plan an author's week where the stories told highlight the work of a particular author and celebrate the contributions he/she has made to children's literature. Guest authors can also be invited, interviewed and asked to share a story orally with the class. The children can publish their own narratives and later share these orally with others.

Trips to an annual storytelling festival can be arranged, along with visits to a seniors' home or hospital where students can tell their stories to other members of the community. The possibilities are endless, but one thing is certain — encouraging students to participate in activities designed to extend their appreciation of stories told aloud fosters a lasting interest in literature.

Organizing around Other Themes and Genres

The theme of Multiculturalism is just one integrated approach that can be used to teach the art of storytelling in the classroom. A unit on the Middle Ages may provide learners with additional opportunities to engage in storytelling experiences by recounting legends from around the world during the Medieval period. A study of the environment or aboriginal peoples can involve learners in retelling native tales from long ago. Learning about ancient civilizations from around the globe enables students to orally share myths from Asia, Africa, Greece, Rome, South and Central America (e.g., Aztec, Inca) as well. Storytelling experiences can also be developed around a fairy tale unit or fantasy theme where students share imaginative stories from all over the world.

Extending the Story Experience

- Dramatize scenes from a story previously heard.
- Make puppets.
- Use puppets to retell a story in a puppet theatre.
- Use a flannel board and felt-made characters, props and symbols to retell a story.
- Compare traditional narratives with modern versions of stories.
- Depict favorite scenes in visual arts activities.
- Recreate powerful story images using different art forms (drama, dance, music, visual arts).
- Prepare cooperative group stories.
- Participate in choral reading/speaking performances.

Stories are part of the fabric of our lives and shape the way we view the world. There is a treasure chest of tales waiting to be told that will bring pleasure and enchantment to audiences of all ages.

Storytelling in the classroom supports learning and should be an intricate part of the school curriculum. Many positive social, emotional and intellectual rewards can be gained by offering children the time, space and opportunity to share their oral stories. These experiences provide a meaningful context for the development of knowledge and language skills that support literacy across the curriculum.

Students, themselves, enjoy the art of storytelling and the transforming power, mysterious elements and sheer excitement that accompanies it. The comments shown here illustrate the enthusiasm shared by participants involved in this traditional art form.

Storytelling opens your mind to new things. It makes me happy to hear stories from different places.

David, Age 11

I like being a storyteller because for once I can change my voice and use my imagination. I can make it a scary story, a happy story or maybe a sad story.

Joshua, Age 11

"I like storytelling…it makes me feel like I'm actually part of the story…in the story…by using my imagination. Also, it's fun listening to different people tell stories. I get ideas for when I tell my own.

Bismattie, Age 11

CHAPTER SEVEN

Assessment and Evaluation

In this period of accountability, assessment and evaluation play a vital role in the teaching and learning process. A variety of tools and techniques can be used to assess and evaluate student achievement. During assessment, information is gathered about students using different methods to determine whether they have achieved the required outcomes, objectives or learning expectations. During evaluation, information about student achievement is compiled from different sources and used to make judgements and place a value (e.g., produce a grade) on students' work and progress. A combination of assessment strategies and evaluation methods should be used in order to develop a holistic profile of each student. These tools can provide insight into the knowledge, skills and attitudes acquired by learners throughout the school year as they engage in comprehensive language learning projects such as those outlined in this book.

Types of Assessment and Evaluation

Diagnostic Assessment

Diagnostic assessment occurs at the beginning of the school year, semester, term, unit of study or at another period of time throughout the school year when students may be experiencing difficulty. This form of assessment enables teachers to identify students' background knowledge, interests, skills, learning styles, strengths and needs in order to develop appropriate learning activities and programs. Various approaches to assessment (e.g., observations, anecdotal notes etc.) are used for reporting but not used for grading purposes.

Formative Assessment

Formative assessment occurs throughout the course of a unit, term, semester or school year. This form of assessment is used to determine learners' progress, improve individual student performance and modify instruction in order to reflect the needs of the class. Various approaches to assessment (e.g., teacher, self and peer assessments, checklists etc.) are used for instructing and reporting purposes. The results of formative assessment are combined with summative evaluation to produce a mark or grade.

Summative Evaluation

Summative evaluation occurs at the end of a unit, course, activity, term, semester or period of time. This form of evaluation is used to measure a student's achievement, understanding of content/concepts and skill development. Combined with other methods of assessment and evaluation, it can also be used to determine program effectiveness and the degree to which learning expectations, outcomes and objectives have been met. Various approaches to evaluation (e.g., performance assessments, tests and examinations etc.) are used for both reporting and grading purposes.

Methods of Assessment and Evaluation

In the wake of standardized testing, assessment and evaluation of student performance have become more formalized. When standardized testing drives curriculum alone, students may feel pressured to perform and the results may not be a true indication of their overall ability. Using a variety of methods and criteria to measure student achievement can motivate learners to produce a higher quality of work and reach a standard of excellence of which they can feel proud.

In order to ensure that effective methods are used to assess and evaluate student performance, teachers should employ a variety of tools and techniques. Apart from being varied, these procedures should reflect the required outcomes, program objectives or learning expectations established in the curriculum. In order to develop reliable and fair measures of student achievement, teachers should also take into account the various cultural, ethnic and linguistic backgrounds of the students, along with their prior experiences and special needs. These methods might include:

- Anecdotal notes;
- Observations;
- Checklists;
- Rating scales (analytic scales);
- Marking schemes;
- Presentations and demonstrations;
- Projects;
- Essays;
- Performance assessments;
- Rubrics and performance charts;
- Tests, examinations and quizzes;
- Interviews and conferences;
- Inventory sheets and surveys;
- Self, peer and group evaluations;
- Portfolios and student profiles.

Throughout the school year, teachers and students can work together to assess and evaluate:

- Background knowledge, skills and attitudes;
- Final products;

- Culminating activities;
- The learning process;
- Task completion;
- Participation;
- Cooperation with others;
- Group work;
- Effort/commitment to the task.

By employing different strategies outlined in this chapter, teachers can gain insight into the knowledge, skills, attitudes, interests, behaviors, strengths and needs of individual students in order to develop comprehensive and consistent profiles of learners in their classroom.

Evaluating Language Learning Projects

When selecting the assessment and evaluation methods to be used with the language learning projects in this book, teachers may choose from tools that have been specifically developed for each chapter — as outlined in the overview chart on the next page and provided in the subsequent pages — or incorporate effective strategies of their own.

OVERVIEW OF ASSESSMENT AND EVALUATION

Chapter Title	Assessment/Evaluation Tools Provided	Description	General Knowledge/ Skills
Examining the Novel	Novel Study Evaluation Sheet Reading Assessment Form	• A summative marking scheme used by the teacher to evaluate a variety of responses to reading. • A formative assessment used by the teacher to record observations and anecdotal notes about a student's reading behaviors.	• Understand the characteristics of novels. • Identify basic elements of story. • Read and respond to novels in a variety of ways.
Publishing Picture Books	Picture Book Evaluation Sheet Writing Self-Evaluation Checklist	• A summative marking scheme used by the teacher to evaluate the production of a picture book. • A formative checklist used by the student to assess his/her writing development.	• Understand the characteristics of picture books. • Investigate various conventions for writing a story. • Apply knowledge of story elements to writing a picture book. • Use the stages of the writing process.
Studying Traditional Folklore	Myth Teacher/Student Evaluation Sheet Legend Writing Conference Sheet	• A summative rating scale used by the teacher, student and/or peer to evaluate a published myth. • A formative/summative conference form used by the teacher to record observations and anecdotal notes during the writing process and about the published legend.	• Understand the characteristics of myths and legends. • Extend knowledge of story elements (especially character). • Apply knowledge of story elements and narrative structure to other genres.
Creating Poetry	Poetry Reading Checklist Poetry Writing Evaluation Form	• A formative checklist used by the teacher to assess a student's poetry reading behaviors. • A summative rating scale used by the teacher to evaluate a student's poetry writing.	• Understand the characteristics of different forms of poetry. • Read and respond to poetry in a variety of ways. • Produce poetry using various forms and conventions.
Investigating Non-Fiction	Research Skills Rubric News Item Rubric	• A formative/summative rubric used by the teacher to evaluate a student's use of the research process based on achievement level performance criteria. • A formative/summative rubric used by the teacher to evaluate news items based on achievement level performance criteria.	• Understand characteristics of non-fiction and newspapers. • Conduct research using non-fiction resources. • Use steps in the research process to gather information and develop inquiry skills. • Present research findings in the form of news items (e.g., report).
Recounting Oral Stories	Story Map Checklist Storytelling Presentation Self/Peer/Teacher Evaluation Form	• A summative checklist used by the teacher to evaluate a completed story map. • A summative marking scheme used by the teacher, student and/or peer to evaluate a storytelling presentation.	• Listen to stories from a variety of sources. • Select a story to tell. • Produce a story map. • Tell stories aloud in an engaging way.

Novel Study Evaluation Sheet

Name:_____   Date:_____

Title of the Novel:_____

Criteria	Actual Mark	Possible Marks
Character Awareness/Development • Demonstrates understanding of characters and relationships • Draws comparisons • Makes reference to new characters		10
Explanation of Plot • Includes story details • Contains accurate/relevant information • Understands cause and effect relationships		10
A Sense of Setting • Demonstrates awareness of time, place, season, historical period, change in location		5
Understanding of Theme • Recognizes central meaning of the story • Selects main idea		5
Analysis of Problems/Conflicts • Identifies story conflicts • Predicts outcomes • Distinguishes fact and opinion		10
Provides Solutions • Makes judgements • Offers advice to the characters		10
Language Usage and Vocabulary Development • Uses appropriate word choices in responses • Understands new vocabulary		5
Evidence from the Text • Uses evidence (i.e., details about story elements, examples) from the text to support ideas and develop responses		10
Reading Responses • Responds to literature in a variety of ways (e.g., drama, storytelling, art, media, writing-in-role) • Raises questions and answers those previously raised • Makes predictions and alters them based on new evidence		10
Relates Literature to Own Experiences • Shares personal reactions and relates story events to own personal life • Describes emotions and opinions following significant story events		10
Literary Discussions • Participates in book talks, literature circles • Shares reactions, interpretations, predictions		10
Expands on the Text • Draws inferences • Makes conclusions • Analyzes and synthesizes information • Extends learning experiences		5
Comments: **Total Marks:**		**100**

Reading Assessment Form
Observations and Anecdotal Notes

Name of Student:_____   Date:_____

<table>
<tr><td colspan="2">Activity Observed (Circle One):   Read-Aloud Experience

Independent Reading   Guided Reading   Literary Discussion (e.g., reading conference)

Reading Response Activity:_____   Other:_____</td></tr>
</table>

Criteria	Strengths/Area(s) for Improvement
Reading for Meaning • Uses different reading strategies to make sense of texts (rereads to clarify meaning, uses context clues/phonics)	
Understanding of Story Elements • Identifies plot, setting, character, theme and other narrative elements correctly • Provides evidence from the text (e.g., gives examples, supporting details)	
Skill Development • Makes inferences, judgements and predictions based on reading material • Interprets and analyzes content • Examines issues through inquiry (e.g., raises questions etc.)	
Reading Responses • Demonstrates knowledge of story elements in reading responses • Uses imagination and creativity to respond to novels in a variety of ways	
Participation • Participates in different reading experiences independently and with others (e.g., conference) • Relates reading material to own life experiences and shares personal reactions and opinions	
Appreciation for Literature • Reads for a variety of purposes (e.g., enjoyment) • Recognizes the value of literature experiences	
Other	

Picture Book Evaluation Sheet

Name: _____   Date: _____

Title of Picture Book: _____

Marking Scheme: (Letter Grades)	**A** Excellent	**B** Good	**C** Satisfactory	**D** Needs Improvement
Criteria			**Grade**	
Knowledge and Use of the Writing Process • Follows the steps in the writing process (pre-writing activities, rough drafts, editing/revision, final copy)			A B C D	
Content • Includes relevant information, supporting facts and details			A B C D	
Organization of Ideas • Develops ideas fully and presents them in a logical sequence • Follows format of a picture book (text and illustrations) • Includes an introduction, body and conclusion			A B C D	
Genre Features • Includes characteristics of picture books and elements of story (characters, setting, plot, theme)			A B C D	
Imagination and Creativity • Includes innovative ideas • Demonstrates originality			A B C D	
Writing Strategies/Techniques • Uses a variety of effective strategies to construct story components (beginnings, endings, dialogue)			A B C D	
Application of Language Conventions • Applies knowledge of spelling, grammar, punctuation etc. rules consistently and accurately			A B C D	
Diction and Word Usage • Uses descriptive words and wide vocabulary to express ideas			A B C D	
Sentence Structure • Uses a variety of sentence structures and patterns (e.g., complete, simple, complex)			A B C D	
Illustrations • Uses a variety of art techniques and materials to create illustrations • Reflects story content in pictures			A B C D	

Comments:

Writing Self-Evaluation Checklist

Name:_____   Date:_____

I have worked through the following stages of the writing process:

❏ Pre-writing Activities   ❏ First Draft   ❏ Second Draft   ❏ Proofreading

❏ Brainstorming Ideas   ❏ Revising   ❏ Editing   ❏ Publishing
   (e.g., outline, story grammar)

I need to work on the following stages of the writing process:

❏ Pre-writing Activities   ❏ First Draft   ❏ Second Draft   ❏ Proofreading

❏ Brainstorming Ideas   ❏ Revising   ❏ Editing   ❏ Publishing
   (e.g., outline, story grammar)

I have written for the following purposes:

❏ to inform   ❏ to entertain   ❏ to persuade

❏ to explain   ❏ to record   ❏ to retell

I need to try writing for the following purposes another time:

❏ to inform   ❏ to entertain   ❏ to persuade

❏ to explain   ❏ to record   ❏ to retell

I have produced different types of writing, including the features of these genres:

❏ myth   ❏ legend   ❏ non-fiction (e.g., report)

❏ narrative   ❏ poetry   ❏ other _____
   (e.g., picture book)

I need to produce different types of writing, including the features of these genres, another time:

❏ myth   ❏ legend   ❏ non-fiction (e.g., report)

❏ narrative   ❏ poetry   ❏ other _____
   (e.g., picture book)

I have improved the following aspects of my writing:

❏ spelling   ❏ punctuation   ❏ organization of ideas

❏ vocabulary   ❏ grammar   ❏ other _____
   (e.g., using new words)

I still need to develop the following aspects of my writing:

❏ spelling   ❏ punctuation   ❏ organization of ideas

❏ vocabulary   ❏ grammar   ❏ other _____
   (e.g., using new words)

I have improved the following story elements in my narrative writing:

❏ beginnings   ❏ setting   ❏ theme, moral/lesson

❏ characters   ❏ plot (action, events)   ❏ endings

I stiil need to develop the following story elements in my narrative writing:

❏ beginnings   ❏ setting   ❏ theme, moral/lesson

❏ characters   ❏ plot (action, events)   ❏ endings

Myth Teacher/Student Evaluation Sheet

Student's Name:_____   Date:_____

Title of Myth:_____

Rating Scale:	5	4	3	2	1
	Excellent	Good	Satisfactory	Limited	Needs Improvement

Criteria	Self/Peer	Teacher
Knowledge and Use of the Writing Process • Follows the steps in the writing process (pre-writing activities, rough drafts, editing/revision, final copy)	5 4 3 2 1	5 4 3 2 1
Content • Includes relevant information and supporting details	5 4 3 2 1	5 4 3 2 1
Organization of Ideas • Develops ideas fully and presents them in a logical sequence • Follows narrative style of traditional folklore • Includes an introduction, body and conclusion	5 4 3 2 1	5 4 3 2 1
Purpose • Writes for specific purpose(s) (e.g., to explain, entertain, inform readers etc.) • Communicates lesson/moral clearly	5 4 3 2 1	5 4 3 2 1
Genre Features • Includes characteristics of myths (mythical character, complex plot, moral/lesson etc.)	5 4 3 2 1	5 4 3 2 1
Imagination and Creativity • Includes innovative ideas and originality	5 4 3 2 1	5 4 3 2 1
Visual Presentation and Style • Arranges story content in paragraphs • Makes narrative easy to read (includes a title, indents paragraphs, makes sure format is equally spaced with margins)	5 4 3 2 1	5 4 3 2 1
Application of Language Conventions • Applies knowledge of spelling, grammar, punctuation etc. rules consistently and accurately	5 4 3 2 1	5 4 3 2 1
Diction and Word Usage • Uses descriptive words and wide vocabulary to express ideas	5 4 3 2 1	5 4 3 2 1
Sentence Structure • Uses a variety of sentence structures and patterns (e.g., complete, simple, complex)	5 4 3 2 1	5 4 3 2 1
Comments: **Total Marks:**	/50	/50

Legend Writing Conference Sheet

Name:_____   Date:_____

Title of Legend:_____

Criteria	Anecdotal Notes/Comments
Knowledge and Use of the Writing Process • Follows the steps in the writing process (pre-writing activities, rough drafts, editing/revision, final copy)	
Content • Includes relevant information, supporting details and actual facts	
Organization of Ideas • Develops ideas fully and presents them in a logical sequence • Follows narrative style of traditional folklore • Includes an introduction, body and conclusion	
Purpose • Writes for different purposes (e.g., to explain, entertain, inform readers etc.) • Communicates messages clearly	
Genre Features • Includes characteristics of legends (legendary character, goal/conflict, moral/lesson etc.)	
Imagination and Creativity • Includes innovative ideas • Demonstrates originality	
Visual Presentation and Style • Arranges story content in paragraphs • Makes narrative easy to read (includes a title, indents paragraphs, makes sure format is equally spaced with margins)	
Application of Language Conventions • Applies knowledge of spelling, grammar, punctuation etc. rules consistently and accurately	
Diction and Word Usage • Uses descriptive words and wide vocabulary to express ideas	
Sentence Structure • Uses a variety of sentence structures and patterns (e.g., complete, simple, complex)	

Poetry Reading Checklist

Name:_____   Date:_____

The student:	Always	Sometimes	Never
Participates in choral reading and/or choral speaking poetry experiences	❑	❑	❑
Uses voice expressively to convey meaning, mood, feelings and intent	❑	❑	❑
Uses voice, sound effects and movement to read poetry aloud	❑	❑	❑
Alters elements of timing, tempo, tone and volume to make reading more effective	❑	❑	❑
Experiments with gestures and symbols	❑	❑	❑
Uses principles of variety and unity	❑	❑	❑
Demonstrates control of voice (e.g., projection and enunciation)	❑	❑	❑
Revises and rehearses performance with others	❑	❑	❑
Demonstrates awareness of the audience (e.g., by making appropriate selections)	❑	❑	❑

Comments:

Poetry Writing Evaluation Form

Name:_____   Date:_____

Rating Scale:	5 Excellent	4 Good	3 Satisfactory	2 Limited	1 Needs Improvement

The student:					
Experiments with different poetic forms (e.g., pattern, rhyming, free verse etc.)	5	4	3	2	1
Incorporates features common to the format used (e.g., cinquain, limerick etc.)	5	4	3	2	1
Employs different stylistic and literary devices (e.g., simile, metaphor, contrast etc.)	5	4	3	2	1
Uses descriptive language	5	4	3	2	1
Conveys emotions, ideas, mood and meaning effectively	5	4	3	2	1
Expresses thoughts with clarity (uses clear word choices)	5	4	3	2	1
Uses vocabulary and structures to evoke imagery	5	4	3	2	1

Comments:

Research Skills Rubric

Student's Name:_____   Date:_____

Research Topic:_____   Achievement Levels: (highlighted below)

Research Skills	Level 1	Level 2	Level 3	Level 4
Selects a realistic topic	Shows limited ability	Shows some ability	Shows general ability	Shows consistent and thorough ability
Formulates research questions with a clear focus	Shows limited ability	Shows some ability	Shows general ability	Shows consistent and thorough ability
Locates relevant information from a variety of primary and secondary sources	Requires assistance	Requires some assistance	Requires limited assistance	Requires little or no assistance
Understands new information using background knowledge and other reading strategies	Shows limited understanding	Shows some understanding	Shows general understanding	Shows consistent and thorough understanding
Records relevant information on research topic	Unable to record	Somewhat able to record	Generally able to record	Always or almost always able to record
Organizes research information using different strategies (e.g., outlines, concept maps etc.)	In a limited way	In a somewhat satisfactory way	In a satisfactory way	In a thorough way
Analyzes, synthesizes and summarizes information from reference materials and research notes	Shows limited ability	Shows some ability	Shows general ability	Shows consistent and thorough ability
Presents research information using different forms of writing and methods of communication (oral, media, graphic, pictorial, other)	Few methods used	Some methods used	Several methods used	A variety of methods used
Notes references and records bibliographic information accurately	With several errors and/or omissions	With some errors and/or omissions	With few errors and/or omissions	With virtually no errors and/or omissions

Comments:

News Item Rubric

Student's Name:_____   Date:_____

Topic:_____   Title of News Item(s):_____

Type of News Item(s):_____   Achievement Levels: (highlighted below)

Criteria	Levels of Achievement			
	Level 1	**Level 2**	**Level 3**	**Level 4**
Purpose/Focus • Clarity of purpose and ideas • Awareness of audience and task	Unclear Minimal awareness	Somewhat clear Some awareness	Generally clear General awareness	Very clear Strong awareness
Organization • Development of ideas • Sequence of information	Minimal development Lacks sequence	Some development Some sequence	Good development Generally logical sequence	Excellent development Complex and logical sequence
Content • Knowledge of topic and accuracy of information • Facts, examples and supporting details	Minimal knowledge and accuracy Inevident	Limited knowledge and accuracy Somewhat evident	Good knowledge and accuracy Mostly evident	Solid knowledge and accuracy Strongly evident
Form/Layout • Forms of news items used in writing • Textual and visual features of news items (e.g., headline, photo caption etc.)	Few forms used Mostly inaccurate and inevident	Some forms used Somewhat accurate and evident	Several forms used Generally accurate and evident	A variety of forms used Clearly accurate and evident
Language Usage, Grammar, Mechanics • Vocabulary (word choices) • Sentence structure • Grammar • Spelling, punctuation, capitalization	Mostly inappropriate Several errors and/or omissions	Somewhat appropriate Some errors and/or omissions	Generally appropriate Few errors and/or omissions	Consistently appropriate Practically no errors and/or omissions

Comments:

Story Map Checklist

Name:_____

Title of Story:_____

Genre Type:_____

Country of Origin: _____

Does the story map …	Yes	No
Demonstrate sequence?	❑	❑
Contain narrative elements? (e.g., evidence of character, setting etc.)	❑	❑
Develop logically?	❑	❑
Demonstrate student's understanding of narrative forms and story structures?	❑	❑
Reveal student's personal interpretation of story events?	❑	❑
Present content in an attractive and interesting way?	❑	❑

Comments:

Storytelling Presentation
Self/Peer/Teacher Evaluation Form

Name of Storyteller:_____   Date:_____

Story Title:_____

Type of Evaluation (Circle One):   Self   Peer   Teacher

Name of Evaluator:_____

Marking Scheme: (Letter Grades)	A Excellent	B Good	C Satisfactory	D Needs Improvement
Criteria				**Grade**
Story Selection • Selects an appropriate story to share with others and understands the story content				A B C D
Story Development • Begins the story in an interesting way and describes events in sequence • Develops story logically with no gaps and presents ending clearly				A B C D
Language • Uses interesting language and descriptive word choices — demonstrates vocabulary development				A B C D
Voice • Speaks clearly and expressively, and varies pitch, volume, tone and pace of voice • Uses pauses and silences for effect when appropriate				A B C D
Expressions • Uses facial expressions and other drama techniques (e.g., change of voice) to make the story more interesting				A B C D
Gestures • Incorporates actions, movements and symbols during the presentation				A B C D
Style/Approach • Presents the story in a creative or original way (e.g., uses costumes, props, symbols etc.)				A B C D
Presentation Skills • Uses proper posture, appears calm, demonstrates confidence, shows enthusiasm and enjoys the experience				A B C D
Audience Awareness • Looks at the audience and maintains eye contact with listeners				A B C D
Audience Participation • Involves the audience physically and/or vocally in the storytelling (e.g., repeats a word or phrase) • Responds to the audience's involvement and reactions				A B C D

Comments:

Professional References

Applebee, A. *The Child's Concept of Story: Ages 2 to 17*. Chicago, IL: The University of Chicago Press, 1976.

Appleyard, F., and G. Leitenberg. *Basically Right. English: Intermediate and Senior Divisions*. Ontario Ministry of Education, 1984.

Artell, M. *How to Create Picture Books: A Step-by-Step Guide for Young Authors and Illustrators*. Palo Alto, California: Monday Morning Books, 1994.

Atwell, N. *In the Middle: Writing, Reading and Learning with Adolescents*. Portsmouth, NH: Heinemann, 1987.

Barton, B. *Tell Me Another*. Markham, ON: Pembroke Publishers, 1986.

Barton, B., and D. Booth. *Stories in the Classroom*. Markham, ON: Pembroke Publishers, 1990.

Booth, D., and B. Moore. *Poems Please! Sharing Poetry with Children*. Markham, ON: Pembroke Publishers, 1988.

Booth, D., and G. Oglan. *Writing Sense: A Teacher's Source Book* (Level 4 and Level 6). Toronto: MeadowBooks Press, 1996.

Booth, D., and Swartz, L. *Novel Sense* (Level 4). Toronto: MeadowBooks Press, 1996.

Bosma, B. *Fairy Tales, Fables, Legends and Myths: Using Folk Literature in Your Classroom*. New York: Teacher's College Press, 1987.

Cassady, M. *Storytelling: Step by Step*. San Jose, CA: Resource Publications, 1990.

Chambers, D. *The Oral Tradition: Storytelling and Creative Drama*. Dubuque, Iowa: W.M.C. Brown Company Publishers, 1977.

Colwell, E.H. *Storytelling*. Oxford: The Thimble Press, 1991.

Cornfield, R.J., et al. *Making the Grade: Evaluating Student Progress*. Scarborough, ON: Prentice-Hall Canada, 1987.

Cullinan, B.E., et al. *Three Voices: An Invitation to Poetry across the Curriculum*. Portland, Maine: Stenhouse; Markham, ON: Pembroke Publishers, 1995.

Daniels, H. *Literature Circles: Voice and Choice in the Student-Centered Classroom*. Portland, Maine: Stenhouse; Markham, ON: Pembroke Publishers, 1994.

Dias, P. "Literary Reading and Classroom Constraints: Aligning Practice with Theory." *Literature Instruction: A Focus on Student Response*. Ed. Judith Langer. Urbana: NCTE, 1992, pp. 131-62.

Fletcher, R. *What a Writer Needs*. Portsmouth, NH: Heinemann, 1993.

Fletcher, R., and J. Portalupi. *Craft Lessons: Teaching Writing K-8*. Portland, Maine: Stenhouse Publishers, 1998.

Hamilton, M., and M. Weiss. *Children Tell Stories: A Teaching Guide*. Katanah, NY: Richard C. Owen Press, 1990.

Harvey, S. *Nonfiction Matters: Reading Writing and Research in Grades 3-8*. Portland, Maine: Stenhouse Publishers, 1998.

Holland, K., Hungerford, R.A., and S.B. Ernst. ed. *Journeying: Children Responding to Literature*. Portsmouth, NH: Heinemann, 1993.

Howell, T., Ratz, S., and M. Spring. "The Magical World of Picture Books." *Federation of Women Teachers' Association of Ontario Newsletter*. Volume 15, Number 1, 1996.

Jedele, R., and J. Lawson. *Teacher Resources for Retold Classic Myths, Volume 1 and 2*. Iowa: The Perfection Form Company, 1990.

Kooy, M., and J. Wells. *Reading Response Logs: Inviting Students to Explore Novels, Short Stories, Plays, Poetry and More*. Markham, ON: Pembroke Publishers, 1996.

Langer, J. *Envisioning Literature: Literary Understanding and Literature Instruction*. New York: Teachers College Press, 1995.

Mallan, K. *Children as Storytellers*. Portsmouth, NH: Heinemann, 1991.

Ogle, D. "K-W-L: A Teaching Model That Develops Active Reading of Expository Texts." *The Reading Teacher*. Volume 39, 1986, pp. 564-70.

Olgan, G. (ed.), et al. *Writing Sense: Your Writing Skills Handbook* (Student Editions, Book 4 and Book 6). Toronto: MeadowBooks Press, 1996.

Ontario Ministry of Education and Training. *The Ontario Curriculum Grades 1-8 The Arts*. 1998.

Ontario Ministry of Education and Training. *The Ontario Curriculum Grades 1-8 Language*. 1997.

Ontario Ministry of Education and Training. *The Ontario Curriculum: History and Geography, Grades 7 and 8*. 1998. (Implementation Support Materials)

Parsons, L. *Poetry Themes and Activities: Exploring the Fun and Fantasy of Language*. Markham, ON: Pembroke Publishers, 1992.

Phoenix, J. *The Spelling Teacher's Book of Lists: Words to Illustrate Patterns… and Tips for Teaching Them*. Markham, ON: Pembroke Publishers, 1996.

Powell, B. *Their Own Special Shape: Further Approaches to Writing from Classrooms around the World*. Don Mills, ON: Collier-Macmillan Canada, 1976.

Purves, A.C., Rogers, T., and A.O. Soter. *How Porcupines Make Love II: Readers, Texts, Cultures in the Response-Based Literature Classroom*. New York: Longman Publishers, 1995.

Quigley, G. *LISTEN UP! A Festival Storytelling Kit for Kids*. Toronto, ON: The Storytellers School of Toronto, 2000.

Raison G., et al. *First Steps Writing: Resource Book*. Australia: Longman House, 1994.

Ralston, M. *An Exchange of Gifts: A Storyteller's Handbook*. Markham, ON: Pippin Publishing, 1993.

Rosen, B. *And None of It Was Nonsense: The Power of Storytelling in School*. Richmond Hill, ON: Scholastic-TAB Publications, 1988.

Rosen, B. *Shapers and Polishers: Teachers as Storytellers*. London: Collins Educational, 1991.

Rosenblatt, L. *Literature as Exploration*. New York: Modern Languages Association of America, 1983.

Ross, R. *Storyteller* (Second Edition). Ohio: Charles E. Merrill Publishing Company, 1980.

Sawyer, R. *The Way of the Storyteller*. New York: Penguin Books, 1977.

Scarborough Board of Education. "Student Evaluation: Guiding Principles." *How to Design and Teach Using Outcomes*. 1996.

Swartz, L. *Classroom Events through Poetry*. Markham, ON: Pembroke Publishers, 1993.

Swartz, L. *Drama Themes: Completely Revised*. Markham, ON: Pembroke Publishers, 1995.

Winch, G., and G. Blaxell. *The Grammar Handbook for Word-Wise Kids: Basic English Grammar, Punctuation and Usage*. Markham, ON: Pembroke Publishers, 1996.

Zipes, J. *Creative Storytelling: Building Community, Changing Lives*. New York: Routledge, 1995.

Children's Literature

Novels: Relationships Text Set

Bell, W. *Absolutely Invincible*. Toronto: Stoddart Publishing, 1993.

Boyd, C.D. *Circle of Gold*. New York: Scholastic, 1984.

Byars, B. *Coast to Coast*. New York: Bantam Doubleday Dell Books, 1992.

Byars, B. *The Pinballs*. New York: Harper Trophy, 1977.

Byars B. *The Summer of the Swans*. New York: Puffin Books, 1970.

Cleary, B. *Dear Mr. Henshaw*. New York: Dell Publishing, 1992.

Coerr, E. *Mieko and the Fifth Treasure*. New York: Bantam Doubleday Dell Books, 1993.

Coerr, E. *Sadako and the Thousand Paper Cranes*. New York: Bantam Doubleday Dell Books, 1977.

de Angeli, M. *The Door in the Wall*. New York: Bantam Doubleday Dell Books, 1977.

Ellis, S. *Next Door Neighbours*. Toronto: Groundwood, 1989.

Etherington, F. *The General*. Willowdale, ON: Annick Press, 1983.

Fleischman, S. *The Whipping Boy*. New York: Troll Communications, L.L.C., 1986.

Gardiner, J.R. *Stone Fox*. New York: Harper Collins, 1980.

Hamilton, V. *Cousins*. New York: Scholastic, 1990.

Hamilton, V. *The Planet of Junior Brown*. New York: Macmillan Publishing, 1971.

Hughes, M. *Beyond the Dark River*. Toronto: Stoddart Publishing, 1992.

Kinsey-Warnock, N. *The Canada Geese Quilt*. New York: Dell Publishing, 1989.

Lewis, C.S. *The Lion, the Witch, and the Wardrobe*. New York: Harper Trophy, 1978.

Little, J. *The Belonging Place*. Toronto: Penguin Books Canada, 1997.

MacLachlan, P. *Journey*. New York: Delacorte, 1991.

MacLachlan, P. *Sarah, Plain and Tall*. New York: Harper Trophy, 1985.

Myers, W.D. *Somewhere in the Darkness*. New York: Scholastic, 1992.

Naidoo, B. *Journey to Jo'Burg: A South African Story*. New York: Harper Collins, 1986.

Naylor, P.R. *Shiloh*. New York: Dell Publishing, 1991.

Winthrop, E. *The Castle in the Attic*. New York: Bantam Doubleday Dell Books, 1985.

Woodson, J. *Last Summer with Maizon*. New York: Dell Publishing, 1990.

Yarbrough, C. *The Shimmershine Queens*. New York: Random House, 1989.

Yep, L. *Star Fisher*. New York: Puffin, 1992.

Picture Books: Interdependence Text Set

Burrel, C, et al. *The Peaceosaurus*. Toronto: Dasosurus Press, 1989.

Coerr, E. *Sadako*. New York: The Putnam and Grosset Group, 1983.

Dolphin, L. *Neve Shalom. Wahat Al-Salam. Oasis of Peace*. New York: Scholastic, 1993.

Fleming, V. *Be Good to Eddie Lee*. New York: Philomel Books, 1993.

Fox, M. *Whoever You Are*. Harcourt Brace & Company, 1997.

Grant, James P. *I Dream of Peace: Images of War by Children of Former Yugoslavia*. New York: Harper Collins Publishers, 1994.

Grifalconi, A. *The Village of Round and Square Houses*. Boston: Little, Brown and Company, 1986.

Hamanaka, S. *Peace Crane*. New York: Morrow Junior Books, 1995.

James, B. *The Mud Family*. Toronto: Oxford University Press, 1994.

Jeffers, S. *Brother Eagle, Sister Sky: A Message from Chief Seattle*. New York: Dial Books, 1991.

Laurin, A. *Perfect Crane*. New York: Harper and Row Publishers, 1981.

Martenova Charles, V. *The Crane Girl*. Toronto: Oxford University Press, 1992.

Marton, J. *You Can Go Home Again*. Toronto: Annick Press, 1994.

McLean, D. *Steel Drum and Ice Skates*. Vancouver: Douglas & McIntyre, 1992.

Oppenheim, S.L. *The Lily Cupboard*. New York: HarperCollins, 1992.

Perry-Heide, F., and J. Heide Gilliland. *Sami and the Time of Troubles*. New York: Clarion Books, 1992.

Scholes, K. *Peace Begins with You*. Boston: Little Brown and Company, 1993.

Tsuchiya, Y. *Faithful Elephants. A Story of Animals, People and War*. Boston: Houghton Mifflin, 1988.

Uchida, Y. *The Bracelet*. New York: Philomel Books, 1986.

Valgardson, W.D. *Sarah and the People of Sand River*. Vancouver: Douglas & McIntyre, 1996.

Wild, M., and J. Vivas. *A Time for Toys*. Toronto: Kids Can Press, 1991.

Young, E. *Moon Mother*. New York: HarperCollins Publishers, 1993.

Myths and Legends Resources

General Titles

Jaffrey, M. *Seasons of Splendor: Tales, Myths and Legends of India*. New York: Puffin Books, 1985.

Pickels, D.E. *Roman Myths, Heroes and Legends*. Philadelphia: Chelsea House Publishers, 1999.

Sheppard, S. *Myths and Legends from around the World*. Sydney, Australia: Reader's Digest, 1994.

Myths

Anderson, L. *Arion and the Dolphins*. New York: Charles Scribner's Sons, 1978.

Evslin, B. *Hercules*. New York: William Morrow and Company, 1984.

Evslin, B. *Heroes, Gods and Monsters of the Greek Myths*. New York: Bantam Books, 1975.

Evslin, B. *Jason and the Argonauts*. New York: William Morrow and Company, 1986.

Evslin, B. *The Minotaur: Monsters of Mythology*. New York: Chelsea House Publishers, 1987.

Fisher, L.E. *Theseus and the Minotaur*. New York: Holiday House, 1988.

Fisher, L.E. *Gods and Goddesses of the Ancient Maya*. New York: Holiday House, 1999.

Hamilton, V. *In the Beginning: Creation Stories from around the World*. New York: Harcourt Brace & Company, 1988.

Jordan, M. *Myths of the World: A Thematic Encyclopedia*. London: Kyle Cathie, 1993.

Lewis, S. *One-Minute Greek Myths*. New York: Doubleday and Company, 1987.

Lottridge, C.B., and A. Dickie. *Mythic Voices: Reflections in Mythology*. Scarborough, ON: Nelson Canada, 1991.

Malam, J. *Ancient Greece: Gods and Goddesses*. Chicago: Peter Bedrick Books, 1999.

Pickels, D.E. *Egyptian Kings and Queens and Classical Deities*. New York: Chelsea House Publishers, 1998.

Richardson, I.M. *Prometheus and the Story of Fire*. New Jersey: Troll Associates, 1983.

Stark, R. *Mythology: Student Edition*. New Jersey: Educational Impressions, 1986.

Stewart, M. *Creation Stories*. Toronto: Stoddart Publishing, 1989.

Vinge, J.D. *The Random House Book of Greek Myths*. New York: Random House, 1999.

Waldherr, K. *Persephone and the Pomegrate*. New York: Dial for Young Readers, 1993.

Williams, M. *Greek Myths for Young Children*. Massachusetts: Candlewick Press, 1991.

Legends

Africa

Cherry, L. *The Dragon and the Unicorn*. San Diego: Voyager Books, Harcourt Brace & Company, 1998.

Medlicott, M. *The River That Went to the Sky: Twelve Tales Told by African Storytellers*. New York: Kingfisher, 1995.

Wisniewski, D. *Sundiata: Lion King of Mali*. New York: Clarion Books, 1992.

Asia

Chin, C. *China's Bravest Girl*. San Francisco: Children's Book Press, 1993.

Lee, J.M. *The Song of Mulan*. Arden, N.C.: Front Street, 1995.

McCully, E.A. *Beautiful Warrior: The Legend of the Nun's Kung Fu*. New York: Arthur A. Levine Books, 1998.

San Souci, R.D. *The Samurai's Daughter*. New York: Dial Books, 1992.

San Souci, R.D. *Fa Mulan*. New York: Dial Books, 1998.

Troughton, J. *The Monkey and the Water Dragon*. London: Dutton, 1995.

Europe

DePaola, T. *The Knight and the Dragon*. New York: The Putnam and Grosset Group, 1980.

Frost, A. *The Age of Chivalry: Myths and Legends*. Bath, Avon: Cherrytree Books, 1989.

Hastings, S. *Sir Gawain and the Loathly Lady*. London: Walker Books, 1987.

Hayes, S. *Robin Hood*. London: Walker Books, 1989.

Hodges, M. *The Kitchen Knight: A Tale of King Arthur*. New York: Holiday House, 1990.

Hodges, M. *Saint George and the Dragon*. Boston: Little, Brown and Company, 1984.

Howe, J. *The Knight with the Lion: The Story of Yvain*. Boston: Little, Brown and Company, 1996.

Lister, R. *The Legend of King Arthur*. New York: Doubleday, 1988.

Mooser, S. *Young Marian's Adventures in Sherwood Forest*. New York: Meadowbook Press, 1997.

Poole, J. *Joan of Arc*. New York: Alfred A. Knopf, 1998.

Pyle H. *The Legend of King Arthur*. London: Running Press, 1996.

San Souci, R.D. *Young Arthur*. New York: Bantam Doubleday Dell Books, 1997.

San Souci, R.D. *Young Guinevere*. New York: Bantam Doubleday Dell Books, 1993.

San Souci, R.D. *Young Lancelot*. New York: Bantam Doubleday Dell Books, 1996.

San Souci, R.D. *Young Merlin*. New York: Bantam Doubleday Dell Books, 1990.

Talbott, H. *Tales of King Arthur: Excalibur*. New York: Morrow and Company, 1996.

Yolen, J. *Merlin and the Dragons*. New York: Cobblehill Books, 1995.

Zeman, L. *Gilgamesh, the King*. Montreal: Tundra Books, 1992.

India

McKibbon, H. *The Token Gift*. Toronto: Annick Press, 1996.

Sing, R. *The Foolish Men of Agra and Other Tales of Mogul India*. Toronto: Kay Porter Books, 1998.

Judaism

Golden, B. *Journeys with Elijah: Eight Tales of the Prophet*. New York: Gulliver Books, 1999.

Middle East

Carrick, C. *Aladdin and the Wonderful Lamp*. New York: Scholastic, 1989.

Kimmel, E. *The Tale of Aladdin and the Wonderful Lamp*. New York: Holiday House, 1992.

Kimmel, E. *The Tale of Ali Baba and the Forty Thieves*. New York: Holiday House, 1996.

Lewis, N. (ed.) *Stories from the Arabian Nights*. New York: Holt, 1987.

Other Multicultural Legends

Climo, S. *A Treasury of Princesses: Princess Tales from around the World*. New York: HarperCollins Publishers, 1996.

Poetry Books, Anthologies and Children's Collections

Booth, D. *Images of Nature: Canadian Poets and the Group of Seven*. Toronto: Kids Can Press, 1995.

Booth, D. *Till All the Stars Have Fallen: Canadian Poems for Children*. Toronto: Kids Can Press, 1989.

Booth, D. *Voices on the Wind: Poems for All Seasons*. Toronto: Kids Can Press, 1990.

Bryan, A. *Sing to the Sun*. New York: HarperCollins, 1992.

Lee, D. *Garbage Delight*. Toronto: MacMillan of Canada, 1977.

Lee, D. *Lizzy's Lion*. Toronto: MacMillan of Canada, 1984.

Lindbergh, R. *The Circle of Days*. Massachusetts: Candlewick Press, 1998.

Nicholls, J. *Earthways: Poems on Conservation*. New York: Oxford University Press, 1993.

O'Neill, M. *Hailstones and Halibut Bones*. New York: Doubleday and Company, 1961.

Plantos, T. *At Home on Earth*. Willowdale, ON: Firefly Books, 1992.

Rogasky, B. *Winter Poems*. New York: Scholastic, 1994.

Rosen, M. *Mini Beasties*. New York: Puffin Books, 1991.

Stevenson, R.L. *Leaves From a Child's Garden of Verses*. New York: Smithmark, 1992.

Tynes, M. *Save the World for Me*. Porters Lake, NS: Pottersfield Press, 1991.

Yolen, J. *Once Upon Ice and Other Frozen Poems*. Pennsylvania: Wordsong Boyds Mills Press, 1997.

Non-Fiction Books: Past and Present Text Set

Ancient Civilizations

Baquedano, E. *Aztec Inca & Maya*. New York: Alfred A. Knopf, 1993.

Beshore, G. *Science in Ancient China*. New York: Franklin Watts, 1998.

Beshore, G. *Science in Ancient Cultures*. New York: Franklin Watts, 1998.

Cotterell, A. *Ancient China*. New York: Alfred A. Knopf, 1994.

Fister, N., and C. Olexiewicz. *Make History: Ancient Egypt*. Chicago: Lowell House, 1996.

Grant, N. *The Vikings*. New York: Oxford University Press, 1998.

Griffey, H. *Secrets of the Mummies*. Fenn Publishing, 1998.

Harris, J.L. *Science in Ancient Rome*. New York: Franklin Watts, 1998.

Haslam, A., and A. Parsons. *Ancient Egypt*. Toronto: Stoddart Publishing, 1995.

Jacobsen, K.L. *Egypt*. Chicago: Children's Press, 1990.

James, S. *Ancient Rome*. New York: Alfred A. Knopf, 1990.

Mann, E. *The Great Wall*. New York: Mikaya Press, 1997.

Martell, H.M. *Imperial China 221 B.C. to A.D. 1294*. Texas: Raintree Steck-Vaughn Publishers, 1999.

Martell, H.M. *The Kingfisher Book of the Ancient World from the Ice Age to the Fall of Rome*. New York: Scholastic, 1995.

Milton, J. *The Mummies*. New York: Grosset & Dunlap, 1996.

Morley, J. *First Facts about Ancient Egyptians*. New York: Peter Bedrick Books, 1996.

Morley, J. *How Would You Survive as a Viking?* New York: Franklin Watts, 1995.

Schofield, L. (ed.) *Ancient Greece*. New York: Time Life Books, 1997.

Medieval Times

Bedoya, J., et al. *Medieval Times to Today*. New Jersey: Prentice Hall, 1998.

Beshore, G. *Science in Early Islamic Cultures*. New York: Franklin Watts, 1998.

Byam, M. *Arms and Armor*. Toronto: Stoddart Publishing, 1988.

Castelli, G. *The Middle Ages*. New York: Peter Bedrick Books, 1988.

Clare, J.D. (ed.) *Knights in Armor*. San Diego: Random Century Publishing Group, 1992.

Cruxton, J.B., and W.D. Wilson. *Discovering Castle Days*. Don Mills, ON: Oxford University Press, 1998.

Delafosse, C., and Gallimard J. *Cathedrals*. London: Moonlight Publishing, 1995.

Gravett, C. *Eyewitness Books: Castle*. Toronto: Stoddart Publishing, 1994.

Hindley, J. *The Time Traveller Book of Knights and Castles*. London: Usborne Publishing, 1976.

Howarth, S. *What Do We Know about the Middle Ages?* New York: Peter Bedrick Books, 1995.

Husain, S. *What Do We Know about Islam?* New York: Peter Bedrick Books, 1995.

Jacobs, H.H. , LeVasseur, M.L., and Randolph, B. *Medieval Times to Today*. New Jersey: Prentice Hall, 1998.

Kerr, D. *Knights and Armor*. London: Franklin Watts, 1997.

Kerr, D. *Medieval Town*. New York: Franklin Watts, 1997.

Langley, A. *Castle at War: The Story of a Siege*. Toronto: Stoddart Publishing, 1999.

Langley, A. *Eyewitness Books: Medieval Life*. Toronto: Stoddart Publishing, 1996.

Leon, V. *Outrageous Women*. New York: John Wiley & Sons, 1982.

Macaulay, D. *Castle*. Boston: Houghton Mifflin, 1977.

Macaulay, D. *Cathedral*. Boston: Houghton Mifflin, 1973.

Macdonald, F. *How Would You Survive in the Middle Ages?* New York: Franklin Watts, 1995.

Mason, A. *If You Were There: Medieval Times*. London: Marshall Publishing, 1996.

McNeill, S. *The Middle Ages*. New York: Oxford University Press, 1998.

Moktefi, M. *The Arabs in the Golden Age*. Connecticut: MillBrook Press, 1992.

Oakes, C. *Exploring the Past: The Middle Ages*. San Diego: Gulliver Books, 1989.

Platt, R. *Stephen Biesty's Cross-Sections Castle*. Richmond Hill, ON: Scholastic Canada, 1994.

Pofahl, J. *Middle Ages: Everyday Life*. Minnesota: T.S. Denison and Company, 1993.

Steele, P. *Castles*. New York: Kingfisher, 1995.

Steele, P. *Knights*. New York: Kingfisher, 1998.

Wright, R. *Knights*. New York: Franklin Watts, 1991.

Native Studies

Braine, S. *Drumbeat… Heartbeat: A Celebration of Powwow*. Minneapolis: Lerner Publications, 1995.

Cass, J. *Ekahotan, the Corn Grower: Indians of the Eastern Woodlands*. Toronto: D.C. Heath Canada, 1983.

Cass, J. *Mistatin, The Buffalo Hunter: Indians of the Plains*. Toronto: D.C. Heath Canada, 1983.

Cass, J. *Ochechak, The Caribou Hunter: Indians of the Subarctic*. Toronto: D.C. Heath Canada, 1983.

Cass, J. *Oyai, The Salmon Fisherman and Woodworker: Indians of the North Pacific Coast*. Toronto: D.C. Heath Canada, 1983.

Edmunds, H.L. *Native Americans*. Wayland Publishers, 1992.

Garrod, S. *Indians of the Northwest*. Toronto: Fitzhenry & Whiteside, 1994.

Green, J. *Native Peoples of the Americas*. New York: Oxford University Press, 1992.

Haslam, A., and A. Parsons. *North American Indians*. Toronto: Stoddart Publishing, 1996.

Hoyt-Goldsmith, D. *Totem Pole*. New York: Holiday House, 1990.

Keegan, M. *Pueblo Boy: Growing Up in Two Worlds*. New York: Puffin Books, 1991.

Leavitt, R.M. *Micmac of the East Coast*. Toronto: Fitzhenry & Whiteside, 1993.

Livesey, R., and A.G. Smith. *Discovering Canada: Native Peoples*. Toronto: Stoddart Publishing, 1993.

Marshall, I. *The Beothuk of Newfoundland: A Vanished People*. Newfoundland: Breakwater Books, 1989.

Nicholson, R. *The Sioux*. Richmond Hill, ON: Scholastic Canada, 1992.

Regguinti, G. *The Sacred Harvest: Ojibway Wild Rice Gathering*. Minneapolis: Lerner Publications Company, 1992.

Ridington, J. and R. *People of the Longhouse: How the Iroquoian Tribes Lived*. Vancouver: Douglas & McIntyre, 1982.

Roessel, M. *Kinaalda: A Navajo Girl Grows Up*. Minneapolis: Lerner Publications Company, 1993.

Roessel, M. *Songs from the Loom: A Navajo Girl Learns to Weave*. Minneapolis: Lerner Publications Company, 1995.

Shemie, B. *Native Dwellings: The Southwest. House of Adobe*. Montreal: Tundra Books, 1995.

Shemie, B. *Native Sites: The Southeast. Mounds of Earth and Shell*. Montreal: Tundra Books, 1993.

Steedman, S. *How Would You Survive as an American Indian?* New York: Franklin Watts, 1995.

Pioneer Times

Adams, P. *Early Loggers and the Sawmill*. Toronto: Crabtree Publishing, 1981.

Greenwood, B. *A Pioneer Story. The Daily Life of a Canadian Family in 1840*. Toronto: Kids Can Press, 1994.

Greenwood, B. *Pioneer Crafts*. Toronto: Kids Can Press, 1997.

Kalman, B. *A One-Room School*. Toronto: Crabtree Publishing, 1994.

Kalman, B. *Early Christmas*. Toronto: Crabtree Publishing, 1981.

Kalman, B. *Early Health and Medicine*. Toronto: Crabtree Publishing, 1983.

Kalman, B. *Early Settler Children*. Toronto: Crabtree Publishing, 1982.

Kalman, B. *Early Stores and Markets*. Toronto: Crabtree Publishing, 1981.

Kalman, B. *Early Travel*. Toronto: Crabtree Publishing, 1981.

Kalman, B. *Early Village Life*. Toronto: Crabtree Publishing, 1981.

Kalman, B. *Games from Long Ago*. Toronto: Crabtree Publishing, 1995.

Kalman, B. *In the Barn*. Toronto: Crabtree Publishing, 1997.

Kalman, B. *Pioneer Projects*. Toronto: Crabtree Publishing, 1997.

Kalman, B. *The Early Family Home*. Toronto: Crabtree Publishing, 1982.

Kalman, B. *The General Store*. Toronto: Crabtree Publishing, 1997.

Kalman, B. *The Kitchen*. Toronto: Crabtree Publishing, 1990.

Kalman, B. *Tools and Gadgets*. Toronto: Crabtree Publishing, 1992.

Kalman, B., and D. Schimpky. *Old-Time Toys*. Toronto: Crabtree Publishing, 1995.

Mathieu, J. *The Olden Days*. New York: Random House, 1979.

Neering, R., and S. Garrod. *In the Pioneer Home*. Toronto: Fitzhenry and Whiteside, 1978.

Owens, A.M., and J. Yealland. *Forts of Canada*. Toronto: Kids Can Press, 1996.

Stories and Books for Retelling: Multiculturalism Text Set

Alexander S. *Nadia the Willful*. New York: Dragonfly Books, 1983.

Bailey, L. *Mei Ming and the Dragon's Daughter*. Richmond Hill, ON: Scholastic Canada, 1990.

Ballantyne, B. *Wesakejack and the Flood*. Winnipeg: Bain & Cox Publishers, 1994.

Bruchac, J. *Tell Me a Tale: A Book About Storytelling*. New York: Harcourt Brace & Company, 1997.

Candappa, B. *Tales of South Asia: How Things Begin*. Great Britain: Ginn and Company, 1984.

Candappa, B. *Tales of South Asia: Out of This World*. Great Britain: Ginn and Company, 1984.

Climo, S. *The Korean Cinderella*. New York: Harper Collins, 1993.

Heyer, M. *The Weaving of a Dream: A Chinese Folktale*. New York: Viking, 1986.

Hughes, M. *Little Fingerling*. Toronto: Kids Can Press, 1989.

Johnson, R. *Kenji and the Magic Geese*. New York: Simon & Schuster, 1992.

Jones, E. *Tales of the Caribbean: Anansi Stories*. Great Britain: Ginn and Company, 1984.

Jones, E. *Tales of the Caribbean: Stories from History*. Great Britain: Ginn and Company, 1984.

Jones, E. *Tales of the Caribbean: The Beginning of Things*. Great Britain: Ginn and Company, 1984.

Jones, E. *Tales of the Caribbean: Witches and Duppies*. Great Britain: Ginn and Company, 1984.

Keens-Douglas, R. *The Nutmeg Princess*. Toronto: Annick Press, 1992.

Kimmel, E.A. *Three Princes: A Tale from the Middle East*. New York: Holiday House, 1994.

Kurtz, J. *Fire on the Mountain*. New York: Simon & Schuster Books for Young Readers, 1994.

Louie, A. *Yeh-Shen: A Cinderella Story from China*. New York: Philomel, 1982.

Martin Jr., B., and J. Archambault. *Knots on a Counting Rope*. New York: Henry Holt and Company, 1987.

Martin, R. *The Rough-Face Girl*. New York: G.P. Putnam's Sons, 1992.

Milfold, S. *Tales Alive: Ten Multicultural Folktales with Activities*. Charolette, Vermont: Williamson Publishing, 1995.

Mollel, T.M. *The King and the Tortoise*. Toronto: Lester, 1993.

Mollel, T.M. *The Orphan Boy*. Toronto: Oxford University Press, 1990.

Muller, R. *The Magic Paintbrush*. New York: Doubleday, 1989.

San Souci, R. *Sukey and the Mermaid*. New York: Four Winds Press, 1992.

Schroeder, A. *Lily and the Wooden Bowl*. New York: Bantam Doubleday Dell Publishing Group, 1994.

Spagnoli, C. *Judge Rabbit Helps the Fish: A Tale from Cambodia*. Bothell, WA: Wright Group Publishing, 1995.

Spagnoli, C. *Kantjil and Tiger: A Tale from Indonesia*. Bothell, WA: Wright Group Publishing, 1995.

Spagnoli, C. *Oni Wa Soto: A Tale from Japan*. Bothell, WA: Wright Group Publishing, 1995.

Stangis, J. *Grandfather's Rock: An Italian Folktale*. Boston: Houghton Mifflin, 1993.

Steptoe, J. *Mufaro's Beautiful Daughters*. New York: Lothrop, Lee & Shepard, 1987.

Troughton, J. *When Animals Could Talk*. Boston: Houghton Mifflin, 1992.

Yashinsky, D. *Next Teller: A Book of Canadian Storytelling*. Charlottetown, P.E.I.: Ragweed Press, 1994.

Yep, L. *The Rainbow People*. New York: Harper & Rowe, 1989.

Yolen, J. *The Emperor and the Kite*. New York: Philomel, 1988.

Miscellaneous References

Aliki. *A Medieval Feast*. New York: HarperCollins Publishers, 1983.

Sheldon, D. *The Whales' Song*. London: Random House Children's Books, 1990.

Index

Acknowledgements

To:
- My students, whose outstanding work and learning experiences have inspired me to write this book
- Gillda Leitenberg, for recognizing my potential and opening up doors of opportunity
- John Glossop, for sharing his knowledge of children's literature
- Greeba Quigley, for introducing me to the art of storytelling in an enchanting way
- Emma DeTommaso and Joan Fulford, for their mentorship and example
- Vince DePasquale and the many other teachers with whom I have worked, for the teaching and learning projects we have shared
- Jennifer Drope, whose editorial guidance and vision helped shape this book
- Mary Macchiusi, whose energy and commitment empowered this project from start to finish
- My family and friends, for their interest in my writing and encouragement